Collins

need to know?

Outdoor Survival

John Lofty Wiseman

Collins

First published in 2006 by Collins
an imprint of
HarperCollins Publishers
77–85 Fulham Palace Road
London W6 8JB

www.collins.co.uk

A catalogue record for this book is available from
the British Library

Designed and produced by Basement Press
Editor: Nicola Chalton
Designer: Pascal Thivillon
Series design: Mark Thomson
Black and white illustrations: Steve Cross,
Chris Lyon, Andrew Mawson and Tony Spalding
Colour illustrations: Norman Arlott
Front cover photograph: © David Forster/Alamy
Back cover photographs: © from left to right,
Hemera Technologies/Alamy, Corbis, Corbis

ISBN 13 978-0-00-721665 3
ISBN 10 0-00-721665 9

Colour reproduction by Colourscan, Singapore
Printed and bound by Printing Express Ltd,
Hong Kong

Contents

Introduction 6

1   **Survival basics** 12

2   **Making camp** 34

3   **Water and food** 60

4   **On the move** 90

5   **Dangers** 114

6   **Rescue** 142

7   **First aid** 162

Need to know more? 190

Index 191

What is outdoor survival?

Outdoor survival involves being isolated from normal services and supplies: no medical help near at hand, no shops and public transport to rely on, no hotels or guesthouses to drop into when the weather turns bad.

When surviving outdoors you live off the land for all your basic needs: food, water, warmth and shelter. You may choose to live like this, perhaps during a camping trip or a hiking expedition, or you may find yourself with no other option — you are lost, your vehicle breaks down, floods sweep away your home or injury leaves you stranded in a remote and inhospitable environment.

Where could this happen?

You can be isolated anywhere in the world. Arctic ice, desert, tropical rainforest and the open ocean can all involve extreme isolation and associated challenges. Closer to home, a hiking trip in the forests or mountains, camping on moorland or in rugged country with few inhabitants, can also take you far away from modern facilities. Remote countryside draws us with its beauty and offer of escape from hectic life, but it can also be hazardous and inhospitable when things go wrong. Luckily, each one of these environments can be exploited for food, fuel, water and shelter — if you know how.

Who does this affect?

Knowing the skills to survive outdoors is becoming increasingly relevant. Not only are we indulging in more exotic holidays, challenging expeditions and regular hiking, climbing and camping outings, our very mobility means we are more likely to be caught up in natural disasters of some kind or other: severe storms, avalanches, forest fires, even earthquakes. Everyone planning to hike in the countryside should be prepared for anything, and outdoor survival training is the best insurance policy you can take out.

What do you need for outdoor survival?

Survival is as much a mental attitude as a matter of physical endurance and knowledge. Think of survival skills as a pyramid built on the foundation of your will to live. People with a will to live have come through the harshest conditions, even though they might have done everything against the rule book.

Will to live

A will to live means never giving in, regardless of the situation. It is very reassuring to know that there is nothing on this earth that we cannot deal with,

must know

Survival check list
Make sure you are well prepared before you set out:
► Know how to take everything possible from nature and use it to the full.
► Know how to attract attention to yourself so that rescuers may find you.
► Know how to make your way across unknown territory back to civilisation.
► Know how to maintain a healthy physical condition.
► Know how to maintain your morale and that of others in the group.

and there is no place on earth where we cannot survive, provided we have the will to live. Some people have a stronger will to live than others, but we can all improve. You can have all the knowledge and kit in the world, but without the will to live you may still perish.

Knowledge

With a little knowledge, survival is a whole lot easier, and the more knowledge you have the simpler it is to survive. Knowledge breeds confidence and dispels fear; it makes your actions positive and more likely to help rather than hinder a situation. This book is intended to supply the information and skills you need for surviving outdoors. Think of it as a first step. There are suggestions at the end of each chapter for further steps you can take to gain more in-depth knowledge and specialised skills. For example, you may wish to refer to books on mountaineering, sailing or pot-holing, and reading them will be part of your preparatory research before taking up these activities. You can also prepare yourself for a trip by talking to people who have travelled in the area you plan to visit, or survived a difficult situation and have advice to pass on. You can never have enough knowledge before you set out.

Kit

The tip of the pyramid of survival skills is kit. Proper equipment and provisions are common sense, but the difficulty is that you will not necessarily know in advance what the conditions will be and therefore what to equip for. That is where your survival kit (see page 24) will make a tremendous difference — it contains a few key items that you cannot do without if you are surviving off the land, all of which fit into a small tin. A survival pouch (see page 28) contains larger, still essential items. And there are other pieces of equipment you should never leave home without, like a knife (see page 32), compass and radio or phone.

Apart from knowing what to take, you need to understand how to use your equipment and know its capabilities and limitations. Seek the expert advice of people who regularly use the equipment rather than trying to find out by trial and error. You will learn more quickly and expose yourself to less risks.

must know

Practise your skills
It is not enough to know the theory of survival in the wild. You must practise the skills in all conditions until you really master them.

You should also test your equipment thoroughly before setting out. Do this in different conditions so you are more likely to reveal any potential weaknesses. The aim is to avoid finding yourself miles away from anywhere, in the middle of a long hike, with a rucksack, tent or walking boots that are not up to the job.

Applying your knowledge

You must use your own judgement in the application of methods described in this book. The tests for plant foods, for instance, may be your only way of being certain whether a particular fruit or leaf is safe or poisonous. The average person is unlikely to come to any harm if they follow the method carefully, but there is risk involved. Individual responses to poisons vary — even small quantities of toxic substances can be very dangerous to some people. Setting traps can also be very dangerous. They should never be left unsupervised where other people may come to harm.

In learning and practising the skills described here, you must take into account the need to conserve the environment and to avoid cruelty to animals, and to abide by the law. Some of the techniques are intended for a survival situation where a life is at risk and there are no alternative courses of action. The risks involved would be

Warning

Some of the survival techniques described in this book are for use in dire circumstances where the safety of the individuals is at risk. The publishers cannot accept any responsibility for any prosecutions or proceedings brought or instituted against any person or body as a result of the use or misuse of any techniques described or any loss, injury or damage caused thereby. In practising and perfecting these survival techniques, the rights of landowners and all relevant laws protecting certain species of animals and plants and controlling the use of firearms and other weapons must be regarded as paramount.

foolish even to consider taking in normal life. Weighing these risks against each other is part of survival strategy. The final choice is yours and no one else can be blamed if you make the wrong one.

Finally, enjoy the benefits of adapting your skills and surviving in the wild. There is nothing quite like cooking food you have found and prepared yourself, on a campfire built from wood gathered locally; to look at the night sky and confirm your direction from the stars, or check the wind for a change in the weather; to cross a river successfully, negotiate a steep gradient or cut through a jungle. All these activities are enjoyable once you know how. Even if things go wrong, knowing the basics of first aid and how to attract a rescue should bring the confidence you need to pull through.

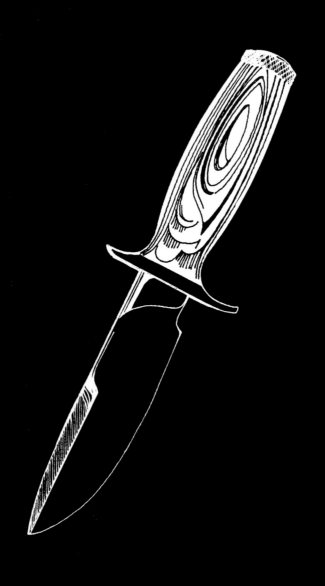

1 Survival basics

Anyone planning an expedition or outdoor adventure should be ready for what may lie ahead. This chapter is about taking the right equipment and preparing yourself for outdoor survival. It introduces the idea of a pocket-sized kit of key survival aids — which should go with you everywhere.

Be prepared

Whether you are going camping, walking or climbing, you should prepare yourself for every eventuality. Good planning and preparation will help you to confront difficulties and dangers that may otherwise spoil your trip, or even threaten your survival.

must know

Essentials for survival
The main elements of survival are food, fire, shelter, water, navigation and medicine. To remember these in order of priority, use the acronym PLAN. This is relevant wherever you are in the world, be it the arctic, desert, jungle, sea or seashore.

P — for Protection
Build a shelter to protect yourself from the elements. Make sure you are away from danger, e.g. do not camp in a flood plain.

L — for Location
When help is needed as a result of an accident, stay within a safe distance of the incident and put out distress signals to draw attention to your position.

A — for Acquisition
Look for water, food and (especially in hot climates) sources of salt. Collect wood and other material for lighting a fire.

N — for Navigation
Good navigation will keep you on track and will often avert a survival situation. If you find yourself separated from the group, always stay where you are.

Survival skills

Almost everywhere nature provides the necessities for survival. In some places the provision is abundant, in others very meagre. It takes common sense, knowledge and ingenuity to take advantage of the resources available. Make sure that you have mastered the survival skills described in this book, and acquired any other specialised knowledge you require for your trip. You will also need determination to succeed — without it, your skills and knowledge will be of little use if you find yourself really up against it.

Research

You can never have too much information about the place you are visiting.
▶ Contact people who know the area, read books and check internet websites for information.
▶ Study your maps carefully and learn about the terrain, e.g. river direction and speed of flow, the height of hills and mountains, the ground conditions along

your chosen route and the network of paths and roads. Maps should be reliable and up-to-date.

▶ Research the local community. Are there customs and taboos you should know about? What facilities are available? Which edible wild plants grow in the area and how are they prepared?

▶ Find out what weather can be expected, the day and night temperatures, the time and height of tides, and the prevailing wind direction and strength.

Health

Make sure you are physically fit enough for what you plan to do. If it is hill-walking, take regular exercise in the weeks before leaving and wear in your hiking boots. Walk to and from work with a bag weighted with sand and get your muscles in condition. Mental fitness is also vital. Are you sure you will cope if things do not go according to plan and you are forced into a survival situation?

Have a thorough medical check and all the necessary injections for the territories through which you intend to travel. Visit your dentist and sort out potential dental problems. Teeth that normally do not hurt can cause pain in cold climates.

Make up a medical kit that will cover all your likely needs and, if organising a group, ensure that any particular individual medical needs are covered.

Vaccinations

Find out from your doctor or travel company which vaccinations (if any) are needed for the places you intend to visit. They may include vaccinations against:

yellow fever
cholera
typhoid
hepatitis
smallpox
polio
diptheria
tuberculosis.

▶ An anti-tetanus injection is advisable for all trips.

▶ Anti-typhoid protection requires three injections over the course of six months.

▶ Anti-malaria tablets must be taken two weeks before your journey, and you should keep taking them for a month after your return.

Avoiding blisters

Break in new boots gradually and harden up your skin with surgical spirit, starting two weeks before you set off. Once on the move, treat blisters as they occur; do not let them become sceptic.

must know

Essential tool
A knife is your most important survival tool. Choose it carefully and keep it in perfect condition.

Equipment

Especially when back-packing, many people initially take too much and have to learn from bitter experience what they really need and what they could have done without. Another common mistake is not testing gear thoroughly before setting out.

Clothing

The correct choice of clothing is very important. Clothing should give good protection and fit well without being restrictive. It must keep you warm and dry while allowing ventilation to the body so you do not overheat.

▶ **Temperate and cold climates:** If heat normally trapped in layers of clothing is continuously being replaced by wind and rain then you are in danger of hypothermia. In cold climates, layering is the answer: you can easily remove or add a layer if it becomes colder, and a waterproof if it rains. Always keep a change of clothing and additional warm garments for when you stop.

▶ **Hot climates:** When on the move wear the least amount of clothing that is practical and avoid walking in waterproofs if you are too hot, as the condensation generated will soak the inner layers. Keep an extra warm layer for cool evenings and nights.

Sleeping bags

There are several types to choose from:

▶ **Hollow-fill, man-made fibre:** A good, inexpensive choice especially if conditions are likely to be wet as it dries out relatively quickly.

▶ **Down-filled:** More expensive, but lighter to carry and gives better insulation than hollow-fill, provided

Equipment check list

Ask yourself the following questions:
▶ How long will I be away? How much food do I need for this period and do I need to carry water?
▶ Have I the right clothing for the climate and enough of it? Is one pair of boots enough or, because of the surface conditions and the amount of walking, should I take a standby pair?
▶ What special equipment do I need for the terrain?
▶ What medical kit is appropriate?

it stays dry. If down gets wet it loses all its insulating properties and is very difficult to dry out.

▶ **Bivouac bag made of Gore-tex™:** This will keep you dry in place of a tent, but in the long term you cannot beat a tent or shelter, which can also be used for cooking and communal activities.

Stow your sleeping bag inside a compression sack to decrease its bulky volume. When in use, place a kip mat under the bag: this insulated waterproof layer will keep you warm and dry.

Packs

Choose the very best back-pack you can afford.

▶ **Strong and comfortable:** It should have tough and fully adjustable webbing, well secured to the pack's frame or fabric. Heavy loads can quickly loosen weak webbing. It must have a comfortable hip belt.

good to know

Carrying weight
The secret of wearing a back-pack is to take the weight securely on the hips — the body's strongest pivot — not on the shoulders and back, which quickly strain and tire.

▶ **External or internal frame?** Internal frames are lighter and make a pack more easy to stow, but external frames are stronger, ensure a more even distribution of the load and are especially useful for awkward or heavy equipment — including, in an emergency, a sick or injured person. A frame adds weight and is more prone to snag on rocky projections or branches, making progress through dense vegetation a little more difficult, but its advantages more than compensate.

▶ **Waterproof:** Choose a pack made from a tough, waterproof fabric, preferably with a lace-up hood inside the main sack to prevent water leaking in and the contents falling out.

Stowing your kit

▶ If you expect to get wet, stow everything in polythene bags.

▶ Pack so you know where everything is and the first things you need are not buried at the bottom. A sleeping bag is probably the last thing you need — pack it first, at the bottom of the pack.

▶ Pack a stove and brew-kit in a side pocket where they are easily accessible when you stop for a rest.

▶ Foodstuffs that can easily squash or melt should be packed in suitable containers. Take into account the extent to which you will be able to live off the land and carry a supply of anything unlikely to be available locally.

G.P.S.

A G.P.S. (Global Positioning System) is an excellent piece of equipment and relatively easy to use. In order to work, the satellite transmission must not have any obstructions in its way, such as a tree branch or building; to receive a clear signal you need to be standing still and out in the open.

When planning your route from a map, choose prominent points that can be used as emergency rendezvous. Enter their coordinates into the G.P.S. to help keep you on track. The equipment will offer information as to where you are in relation to the meeting points and tell you which direction to take to reach them.

A G.P.S. should not replace map-reading skills: use it to confirm your navigation or correct it.

Radios

For a long expedition in remote territory a radio is a necessity. Choose a model with the least number of channels to suit your particular needs. Have a working channel that everyone uses at established times and a priority channel that you can switch to in an emergency. If working with coastguards or forest rangers, make sure your radio is compatible and you know the emergency channel (channel 16). Knowing the frequency of the World Service is also useful. Keep the radio in a safe place, ideally on a person and not in a pack.

► **Signals plan:** Prearrange a signals plan, especially when planning to travel with a large party.

must know

Radio signals
Signals are weaker in a steep gully and valley bottoms. Good signals are received on top of high ground or across water.

Emergency plan

An emergency plan should always be put into operation when two consecutive calls to base are missed. Even when all is well, if you have not been able to make contact this will be treated by base as an emergency. You must return to or stay at the last reported location and await contact. Base will know where you last were and where you planned to go, and the rescue mission can follow.

A signals plan entails having a radio manned at base with scheduled calls morning and evening between party and base. Make sure that the chosen frequencies will work in the areas you are visiting, and that at least two people in the party are familiar with the working of the radio.

In the evening give a situation report to base with your location, what you have done and your future intentions.

In the morning receive an update on weather conditions, a time check and any other information that base can give you. A noon-time call can be used to confirm your position. If you are tackling a dangerous aspect of the expedition you may want to arrange additional calls to base so that in an emergency situation you can call for help and get an immediate response.

Mobile phones

In an emergency a mobile phone can be a life-saver. On expeditions where radios have failed due to bad weather or a difficult location, a mobile phone has been used to raise the alarm. A group on Everest who got into trouble as they started their descent after summitting tried many times to raise base camp by radio without success. The leader then phoned his wife in Hong Kong on a mobile phone and reported their situation. She alerted Kathmandu, who in turn alerted base camp and effected a rescue.

▶ Check the network coverage with the service provider before the trip.

▶ Keep a mobile in the car; they are priceless when help is required and a cigar lighter is a convenient charger for the battery, providing you have an adaptor.

must know

Radios and phones

It takes less power to listen than to transmit, so make your call short and listen for a reply. If nothing is heard do not despair; the transmitting side may be working but not the receiving side. Make calls on the hour. Someone may be picking up your signal so do not give up. Once you hear that rescue is under way, keep your equipment on listening watch.

▶ Charging can be a problem in the wild so use your phone wisely.

Altimeters
In mountainous areas an altimeter is a good idea. Recording the height above sea level of your position, it can help you determine which contour you are on and how far it is to the ridge or summit.

Vehicles
Motor vehicles need special adjustment and modifications to deal with high altitudes and extreme conditions, as well as a thorough overhaul to be sure they are in tip-top working order. You may need tanks for extra fuel and water, together with spares. A tool kit is essential. You should also know basic car maintenance.

Boats and planes
Whether travelling privately or on a commercial service, always take note of the emergency procedures. Remembering them could save your life.

If you are a passenger in a light aircraft ask the pilot about the trip: how long will it take and what sort of ground will you be flying over? Attend to details — they count in an emergency.

Planning
Make plans for every situation, from dealing with accidents to coping with weather and terrain.

Contingency plans
Always prepare contingency plans in case anything goes wrong. What will you do if a vehicle breaks

Flying safety

The safest place on an aircraft is as far back in the tail as possible. In a crash this frequently breaks off and most survivors are from this portion.

Plan for disaster

Many survival sagas begin because of bad nagivaton and people getting lost. Always plan for the worst eventuality and ask yourself if you are up to it.

Water
You cannot carry all your water requirement and you will need to replenish supplies as you travel. Water sources will be a major factor in planning any route.

down, or if weather or ground conditions prove more difficult than anticipated? How will your party regroup if separated? What happens if someone becomes too ill to walk ?

Group planning

For a group expedition get the members together to plan the trip. It may be helpful to nominate people for particular responsibilities: medic, linguist, cook, special equipment, vehicle maintenance, driver, navigator, etc. Ensure that everyone is familiar with the equipment, knows who is carrying what, and that adequate spares are packed — batteries and fuel especially.

Scheduling

In estimating the rate of travel, especially on foot, it is always better to underestimate and be pleasantly surprised by your progress. Pressure to keep to an over-ambitious schedule not only produces tension and exhaustion but leads to errors of judgement and unnecessary risk-taking.

Back-up

Always make sure that someone knows what you are planning to do and by when, and keep them informed at prearranged stages so that failure to make contact will set alarm bells ringing. If you are hiking in the hills, inform the police and local mountain rescue centre. Tell them your proposed plan and give times of departure and expected arrival. If touring by car, log the route with the respective motoring organisation. If sailing, check in with the coastguard and port authorities.

Preparing for the unexpected

Even careful planning cannot prepare you for some of the things that may happen while you are on your trip, but you still need to be ready for them and to react appropriately.

You may wonder how to prepare for things you do not expect: preparing for expected difficulties seems hard enough, so what chance is there of equipping yourself for totally unknown events?

The best preparation you can make for the unexpected is to have mastered a range of survival skills and be ready to apply them to different circumstances, adapting them to fit the particular needs of each situation. Before the trip, practise your skills under difficult conditions, for example try lighting a camp fire in wet or windy weather, building a shelter in barren surroundings or reading a map and finding your way in the dark.

In addition, you should equip yourself with a few small items that will increase your chances of survival if things go wrong. They will fit inside a small container, which can be slipped into a pocket or bag and carried anywhere. This is your survival kit. If there is an emergency you will be glad you always carry it.

Also take with you a knife and a compact collection of useful items that can be carried on your belt — your survival pouch.

The contents of a survival kit and a survival pouch are described in the following pages. Points to remember when choosing and caring for a knife, your most important survival tool, are given in the final section of this chapter.

When things go wrong

It is often a series of unfortunate events that provides the greatest challenge to careful planning and preparation: the weather deteriorates, the radio is broken, the mobile phone is lost, two people have multiple injuries, you are out of water and you have gone off route. Be ready to respond rapidly and deal with the situation rationally and realistically. You must overcome the tendency to panic.

Survival kit

A few key items can make all the difference in the fight for survival. Collect the things listed below. They can be fitted into a small container, such as a tobacco tin — hardly noticeable when slipped into a coat pocket. Make a habit of always having your survival kit with you.

A survival kit fits into a small tin.

Survival kit maintenance

Polish the inside of the tin lid to make a mirror-like reflecting surface, which can be used for signalling in an emergency. Seal the tin to make it waterproof using a strip of easily-removable adhesive tape.

Regularly check the contents, changing any which deteriorate. Mark all drug containers with use and dosage and an expiry date after which they should be replaced. Pack any free space in the tin with cotton wool, which will keep the contents from rattling and can be used for fire lighting.

Contents

Experience has proved that each item in the survival kit earns its place, though some are more useful in certain circumstances than in others: fish hooks, for instance, may be invaluable in the jungle but useless in a desert. Fire is vital to survival in all situations — the first four items are for making it.

Matches (1)

Waterproof matches are useful but ordinary non-safety matches are less bulky and can be made 'shower-proof' by dipping the heads in melted candle fat. To save space, snap off half of each matchstick. Do not waste matches — use only when improvised firelighting methods fail. Take them from the tin one at a time and replace the lid. Never leave the container open or lying on the ground.

Candle (2)
Invaluable for starting a fire as well as a light source. Shave it square for convenient packing. If made of tallow it is also fat to eat in an emergency or to use for frying, but be sure it is tallow — paraffin wax and some other candles are inedible. Tallow does not store well, especially in hot climates.

Flint (3)
Flints will work when wet and they will go on striking long after you run out of matches. Invest in a processed flint with a saw striker.

Magnifying glass (4)
This can start a fire from direct sunshine and is useful for searching for splinters and stings.

Needles and thread (5)
Several needles, including at least one with a very large eye that can be threaded with sinew and coarse threads. Choose strong thread and wrap it around the needles.

Fish hooks and line (6)
A selection of different hooks in a small tin or packet. Add a few split lead weights. Remember that a small hook will catch both large and small fish but a large hook will only catch big ones. Include as much line as possible — it will also be useful for catching birds.

Compass (7)

A luminous button compass — but make sure you know how to read it, as some small compasses can be confusing. A liquid-filled type is best, but check that it does not leak, has no bubbles in it and is fully serviceable. The pointer is prone to rust. Make sure it is on its pivot and swings freely.

Beta light (8)

A light-emitting crystal, only the size of a small coin but ideal for reading a map at night and a useful fishing lure — expensive but just about everlasting.

Snare wire (9)

Preferably brass wire: 60–90cm (2–3ft) should do. Save for snares, but it could also be used to solve many survival problems.

Flexible saw (10)

This usually comes with large rings at the ends as handles, which should be removed to save space (you can add wooden toggle handles when you need to use the saw). To protect from rust and breakage, cover the saw in a film of grease. Flexible saws can be used to cut even quite large trees (see page 38).

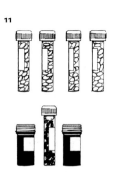

Medical kit (11)

What you include depends upon your own skill in using it. Pack the medicines in airtight containers with cotton wool to prevent rattling.

Surgical blades (12)

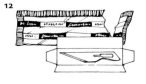

At least two scalpel blades of different sizes. A handle can be made from wood when required.

Butterfly sutures (13)

Use to hold the edges of wounds together.

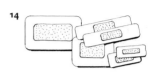

Plasters (14)

Assorted sizes, preferably waterproof, for minor abrasions and keeping cuts clean. They can be cut and used as butterfly sutures for drawing together the edges of a wound.

Condom (15)

This makes a good water-bag — holding 1 litre (2pt).

Useful medicines

The following items will cover most ailments but they are only a guide:

Analgesic: A pain reliever for mild and moderate pain. Codeine phosphate is ideal for toothaches, earaches and headaches. Dose: one tablet every six hours as needed. They can cause constipation as a side-effect so will help in cases of loose bowels. Not to be taken by children, asthmatics or people with liver disorders.

Intestinal sedative: For treating acute and chronic diarrhoea. Immodium is usually the preferred type. Dose: two capsules initially, then one each time a loose stool is passed.

Antibiotic: For general infections. Tetracycline can be used even by people hypersensitive to penicillin. Dose: one 250mg tablet, four times daily, repeated for five to seven days. Carry enough for a full course. If taking antibiotics avoid milk, calcium and iron preparations or other drugs containing aluminium hydroxide.

Antihistamine: For allergies, insect bites and stings (may also help in cases of a bad reaction to a drug). Piriton is recommended in Britain, Benadryl in the USA. Sleepiness is a side-effect of Piriton. Do not exceed recommended dosages or take with alcohol.

Water sterilising tablets: For use where water is suspect and you cannot boil. Follow manufacturers' instructions.

Anti-malaria tablets: Essential in areas where malaria is present. There are types which require only one tablet taken monthly.

Potassium permanganate: Has several important uses. Add to water and mix until the water becomes bright pink and it can be used to sterilise, deeper pink to make an antiseptic and to a full red to treat fungal diseases such as athlete's foot. With sugar, it can be used to light a fire — light it from a spark.

Survival pouch

Essential kit and items you may need in an emergency should be packed together in a survival pouch. Too large to carry in your pocket like the survival tin, a survival pouch should be kept where it can be grabbed quickly, preferably attached to your belt. It should go with you everywhere.

A survival pouch can be carried on your belt.

Pouch

The pouch should be made from tough waterproof material and be large enough to take a mess tin. It should have a positive fastening that will not come undone, and a strong tunnel loop to hold the pouch on your belt.

When on the move your survival pouch should be accessible and not hidden inside your back-pack. It contains fuel, food, survival bag and signalling kit, all packed into a mess tin, which protects the kit and doubles as a cooking utensil. If you fancy a brew or a snack, everything is there, and in an emergency you have essential items to hand.

Anything you use from the pouch must be replenished immediately.

Contents

Warning: the pouch contains matches, solid fuel and flares — all life savers, but dangerous and to be treated with care. Keep these items dry — packed inside watertight containers.

must know

Essential equipment
Some situations are predictable and carrying the proper equipment for dealing with them will minimise the risks.

Mess tin (1)

This is made from aluminium, which is light and strong. A good cooking utensil, it doubles up as protection for the kit that is packed inside it.

Fuel (2)

Ideally you should have solid fuel tablets in their own stove container. The solid fuel tablets are excellent firelighters but use them sparingly and only when a wood fire is difficult to make. The stove unfolds to form an adjustable pot stand and holder for burning fuel.

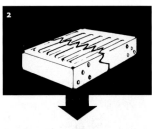

Matches (3)

Pack as many matches as possible sealed tightly in a waterproof container. Use sparingly — you never have enough.

Brew kit (4)

There is nothing like a brew-up to restore morale. Pack tea powder and sachets of dried milk and sugar.

Marker panel

A strip or bar of fluorescent material about 0.3 x 2m (1 x 6ft) used to attract attention in an emergency. One bar signals immediate evacuation and you can form other signals by putting several panels together. When packing use the marker panel to stop items in the pouch from rattling.

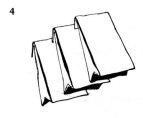

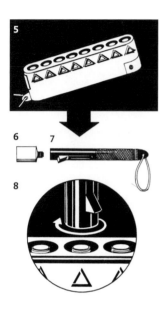

Flares (5-8)

Use signal flares (5) to attract attention, especially in close country. Carry red and green miniflares (6) and a discharger (7) (which is no bigger than a fountain pen). These are explosive so pack carefully. To use, simply remove the discharger and screw it onto the flare (8). Withdraw the flare and point it skywards at arm's length. Pull the trigger to fire. Use with great care and do not waste — keep for emergencies when rescue is needed.

Torch (9)

A small pencil-like torch packs neatly and takes up little room. Alternatively, a light attached to a band around your head is easily packed and allows hands-free use. Store batteries inside the torch in reverse position so they do not run down if accidentally switched on. Lithium batteries are long-lasting and a good choice.

Food (10-13)

Fat is the hardest food to come by when living off the land. The extra calories it provides earn it a place in your kit. Butter, lard or ghee (10) are available in tubes, a convenient way to keep these foods when on the move. Dehydrated meat blocks (11) are nourishing and sustaining, though not very good in flavour. Chocolate (12) is a high-energy food, but does not keep well — check

must know

Matches
Movement against each other can ignite non-safety matches — pack carefully.

regularly. Boiled sweets also provide energy. Salt (13) must be included. A good way to carry it is in tablet form, or, better still, take an electrolite powder which contains vitamins, salt and other minerals required by the body.

Survival bag

A large polythene bag about 200 x 60cm (7 x 2ft) is a lifesaver in the cold. In an emergency get inside the bag to reduce heat loss. The condensation will make you wet, but at least you will be warm. Even better is a heat-insulated bag of reflective material that keeps you warm and solves the condensation problem.

Survival log

Keep a written log of all events. Do not trust your memory. Record discoveries of edible plants and other relevant information about what works and what does not. It becomes a valuable reference and making it helps keep up your morale.

good to know

When brewing
Tea quenches thirst — coffee aggravates it.

10

11

12

13

Knives

A knife is invaluable outdoors. The serious adventurer will always carry one. Knives are dangerous, however, and should never be displayed in tense or awkward circumstances. When flying they should be packed as checked-in luggage — and not in hand baggage — as part of standard anti-hijack procedures.

Folding knife

Choosing a knife

A folding knife can be valuable, provided it has a good locked position. A multi-bladed folding knife is also a useful tool, but if you carry only one knife you need something stronger. A general-purpose blade that does all likely tasks efficiently and comfortably, from cutting branches to preparing vegetables, is the best choice. A blade in a wooden handle is usually the most comfortable type: it will not slip in a sweaty hand and, if the handle is made from a single piece of wood, is less likely to cause blisters than other knives.

General-purpose blade: Handle (a) is ideal: a single rounded piece of wood — the knife tang passes through it and fastens at the end. If the handle breaks the tang can be wrapped with cloth or twine. Handle (b) is only riveted to the tang and would cause blisters. Handle (c) could break at the rivets and the short tang would make it difficult to improvise a handle. The sheath (d) should have a positive fastening and a tunnel belt loop.

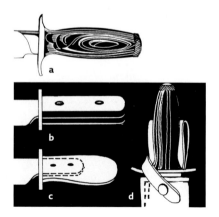

Sharpening a knife

Any sandstone will sharpen tools — a grey, clayey sandstone being best. Quartz, though more rarely found, is good and granite can also be used. Rub two pieces together to make a smooth surface. A double-faced stone with both a rough and a smooth surface is ideal for sharpening. Use the rough surface first to remove burrs, then the smooth one to get a fine edge. The object is to produce an edge that will last and not chip.

To sharpen the blade, hold the handle in the right hand. Use a clockwise circular motion and apply a steady pressure on the blade with the fingertips of the left hand as you push away. Keep the angle constant and the stone wet. Do not drag the blade towards you under pressure: it will produce burrs. Reduce the pressure for a finer edge. Work counterclockwise on the other side.

Blade profile: (a) is too steep and will soon wear, (b) is good and (c) is too fine and might chip.

want to know more?

Take it to the next level...
- ▶ **For more on building a shelter** 36-45
- ▶ **For more on acquiring water, salt and food in the wild** 60-89
- ▶ **For more on first aid** 162-89
- ▶ **For more on navigation** 90-113
- ▶ **For more on signalling and rescue** 142-61

Other sources...
- ▶ Take advice from a reputable outdoor shop on the best clothing and equipment to buy.
- ▶ Learn the phonetic alphabet and use it when spelling out place names on the radio.
- ▶ Ask your doctor for advice on medicines to take with you and other health requirements, including health checks.
- ▶ Mobile phone companies should provide information on network coverage.

must know

You are only as sharp as your knife
Your knife is an important piece of equipment. Always keep it sharp and ready for use, and never misuse it. Do not throw it into trees or into the ground. Keep it clean and, if you do not intend to use it for a while, oiled and in its sheath.

2 Making camp

Once out in the open, you will soon need to look for a safe place to camp. This chapter covers the skills required to construct a comfortable shelter, making use of natural materials from your local surroundings. There are also tips on building and lighting a fire, cooking and hygiene outdoors, and preserving food supplies.

Shelter

Along with food, fire and water, shelter is a basic need for survival. It provides both shade from the sun and a warm, dry environment in cold, wet weather. Making your shelter comfortable will ensure that you sleep and rest well — essential if you are to keep healthy.

must know

Bad places to camp
- Hilltops exposed to wind — move down and look for shelter on the leeside.
- Valley bottoms and deep hollows — may be damp and more liable to frost at night.
- Hillside terraces where the ground holds moisture.
- Spurs that lead down to water, which are often routes to animals' watering places.
- Land liable to flooding.
- Near solitary trees, which attract lightning.
- Near bees' or hornets' nests.

Heavy rainfall

In mountain regions streams can become torrents in minutes, rising as much as 5m (17ft) in an hour.

Where to camp

Look for somewhere sheltered from the wind, on rising ground that has no risk of flooding, and safe from rock falls or avalanches. Ideally you should be close to a supply of firewood and near to water. Pitching camp too close to water, however, may bring troublesome insects, and the sound of running water can hide other noises that might indicate danger, or the sound of search parties. On river banks look for the high water mark and camp a safe distance away. Choose ground that is reasonably flat and free of rocks. In forest areas keep to the edges, where you can see what is going on around you.

Building a shelter

If you are not carrying a tent, you will need to construct a shelter from local materials. For immediate protection, rig up a makeshift shelter: you can construct something more permanent later on. Make use of natural cover — cliff overhangs, gradients, etc — for protection from wind and rain.

Caves

Caves are the most ready-made of shelters. Those situated above a valley are the driest. To close off the entrance use rocks, wattle, logs or turves. Leave gaps for ventilation and for fire smoke to escape. A good fire will usually make animal occupants leave. Allow them an escape route.

must know

Cave dangers
A cave may be inhabited by wild animals, so approach with caution. Check also for possible rock falls inside or outside the cave.

If the cave faces into the wind, build a screen out from both sides, one slightly behind the other, overlapping them to provide an entrance.

Build a fire at the back of the cave. Smoke will go up to the roof, leaving air nearer the floor. If you block the cave entrance make sure you leave a gap for smoke to escape.

Bough shelters

Branches that sweep down to the ground or boughs that have partly broken from a tree can give basic protection from the wind. Weave in other twigs and vegetation to make the cover more dense. Conifers require less weaving-in than broadleaved trees to keep out the rain.

good to know

Avoiding chills
► Never lie or sit on damp ground. Use dry grass or bracken below bedding and dry logs to sit on.
► Increase insulation by wearing layers of clothes. Wear one sock on top of another and stuff dry grass or moss between them.
► Use plastic bags and sheets to make waterproof groundsheets, or lay out large cut sections of birch bark.

Make a similar shelter by lashing a broken-off bough to the base of another branch where it forks from the trunk (a).

Natural hollows

Even a shallow depression will provide protection from wind and can form the basis of a simple shelter. Dig a channel to deflect the flow of water around the hollow, especially if it is on a slope.

Make a roof with branches placed across the hollow to support a light log, against which shorter boughs and sticks can be stacked to give pitch. Fill the gaps with turf.

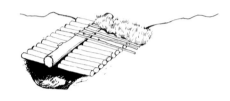

Fallen trunks

A log or fallen tree trunk makes a useful windbreak if it is at the right angle to the wind. Use a small trunk to scoop out a hollow in the ground on the leeward side.

A log also makes an excellent support for a lean-to roof of boughs and turf.

Using a flexible saw

▶ Saw logs and trees so the cut opens (a) rather than closes (b) on the saw, causing it to jam. Do not pull too hard or the saw will break.

▶ Keep the wire taut (c), pulling straight, never at angles (d).

▶ Maintain a rhythm when two people saw. A kink may break the saw (e).

▶ It is usually easier for a single person to cut a log by pulling upwards (f). Prop the log up at an angle to keep the cut open.

▶ Alternatively, to remove a branch, pull down from above (g). This can be dangerous.

▶ High branches can be removed by attaching strings to the saw toggles for extra reach. Be ready to jump clear.

Stone barriers

A shelter is more comfortable if you can sit rather than lie inside. To increase the height of a natural-hollow shelter, build a low stone wall around the perimeter. Seal between the stones with a caulk made from turf and foliage mixed with mud.

Shelter sheet

A shelter can be made using a waterproof poncho, a piece of plastic sheeting or a canvas. Avoid touching the inner surface of the shelter fabric during rain or you will draw water through to the inside.

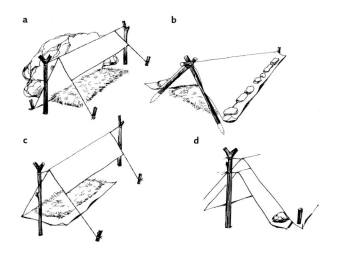

Make use of natural shelter (a) or make a triangular shelter with the apex pointing into the wind (b). If it is long enough, curl the sheeting below you — running downhill to keep out surface water (c). A closely-woven fabric will keep out most rain if set at a steep angle. For double protection, fit one shelter within another (d) — rain will rarely penetrate both layers.

---

must know

Ventilation and drainage
► All shelters must be adequately ventilated to prevent carbon monoxide poisoning and to allow moisture to escape. A minimum of two air holes are needed — one near the top and one near the entrance.
► A run-off channel gouged from the earth around the shelter will help keep it dry.

Useful knots

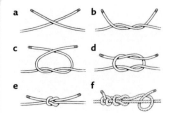

Reef knot: Will hold firm even under strain. Pass the right end over the left (a) and then under it (b). Then take the left over the right (c) and under it (d). Tighten by pulling both strands on each side (e). To be sure, finish by making a half-hitch with the live ends on either side of the knot (f). ('Live ends' are the ends used to tie the knot, the other ends are the 'standing ends'.)

Round turn and two half-hitches: Use to secure a rope to a post. It can take strain from any direction. Carry the rope behind the post, then round again. Bring the live end over and back under the standing end and through the loop thus formed. Tighten and repeat the half-hitch to make the knot secure.

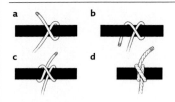

Clove hitch: Effective when strain is perpendicular to the horizontal. Pass the live end over and round the bar (a). Bring it across itself and round the bar again (b). Carry the live end up and under itself, moving in the opposite direction to the standing end (c). Close up and pull tight (d).

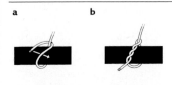

Timber hitch: Use as a start knot for lashings and for dragging or towing heavy logs. Bring the live end round the bar and loosely round the standing end (a). Carry it forward and tuck beneath the rope encircling the bar. Twist it round as many times as comfortably fits (b). Tighten by pulling on the standing end.

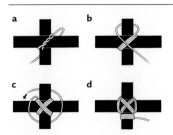

Diagonal lashing: Invaluable for lashing spars together, making rafts, shelters, etc. Make a timber hitch diagonally round both spars (a). Lash both spars with a few turns over the timber hitch, then make a full turn under the bottom spar (b). Lash across the other diagonal, then bring the rope back over one spar and make two or three circuits of the spars above the upper spar and below the lower (c). Finish with a clove hitch (d).

Tepees

The quickest tepee to erect has three or more angled support poles, tied where they cross to make a cone. Cover the tepee with hides, birch bark panels or sheeting. Leave an opening at the top for ventilation.

Wider angles give greater area but are less efficient at shedding rain.

Stick walls and screens

These versatile walls and screens can be used to make one side of a shelter, a door, a heat reflector behind a fire or instead of large rocks to dam a stream. To make a sturdy stick wall, pile two stacks of sticks between uprights driven into the ground and tied at the top. Fill the gap with earth and seal with turf and foliage mixed with mud.

A sturdy stick wall

Coverings

Wattle and woven roof coverings and walls can be made using springy saplings, plant stems, grasses and long leaves. To construct one, first build a framework from less pliable materials, either in situ or as a separate panel to attach later. Tie the main struts in position. Then weave in the more pliant

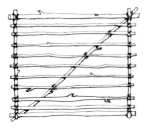

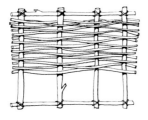

materials. Long grass bunched and woven together creates a barrier for light rain (a). Birch bark cut into shingles makes a more watertight layer: ring a birch tree with even 60cm (2ft) cuts and carefully remove the bark (b); fix pairs of canes or creepers across a frame (c); grip the upper ends of the shingles between the canes, with the lower ends resting on the row below (d).

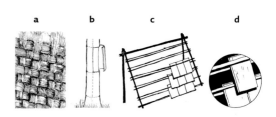

Open lean-to shelter

In a hot climate, an open lean-to shelter may provide all the shelter you need. Lean a framework for a roof on the windward side and attach vertical supports to either side (a). Then weave in more pliable materials between the struts to create a watertight layer, as described above. Site your fire on the side away from the wind and build a reflector (b) opposite to stop the heat from escaping.

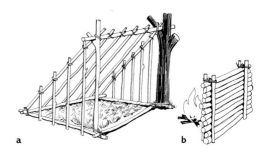

Rope making

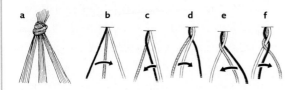

Vines, grasses, nettles, honeysuckle stems, rushes, barks and roots can all be used to make rope or line. Take a bundle of fibres, tie the ends together (a), then twist and plait the strands together (b-f).

Snow trench

In snowy conditions, a trench is quicker to construct than building above ground but is only suitable for one person and for short-term use. It is most effective on a slight slope so cold air collects in the entrance leaving warmer air in the sleeping space above. You need a saw, knife, shovel or machete to cut compacted snow into blocks of approximately 45 x 50cm (18 x 20in) and 10–20cm (4–8in) thick. Start by marking out an area the size of a sleeping bag and cut out blocks the whole width of the trench. Dig down to a depth of at least 60cm (2ft). Along the top of the sides of the trench cut a ledge about 15cm (6in) wide and the same deep. Rest the snow blocks on each side of the ledge and lean them in against each other to form a roof (a). Leave holes for ventilation. Close the windward end with another block or piled snow, leaving a space for air. At the downwind end dig an entrance or use a removable block as a door. Fill any gaps with snow.

Conifer shelter

If you are close to a forest in heavy snow conditions,
you may find shelter in the spaces left beneath the
spreading boughs of conifers, where the snow has
built up around them. A medium-sized tree may
have a space around the trunk (a). A large tree may
have pockets in the snow beneath the branches (b).
Access the space by digging under the tree on the
side away from the wind.

Snow cave

A snow cave is potentially larger than a snow trench.
Dig into a drift of firm snow. Inside the hollow you
have created, dig out three different levels. The
highest level can be used for a fire and the middle
level for sleeping. The lowest level is a trap for cold
air — use it for storage. Drive two holes through the
roof: one to let out smoke and one to ensure
adequate ventilation. Smooth the inside surfaces of
the cave to discourage melt drips, and make a
channel around the internal perimeter to keep any
melt water away from you and your equipment.
Finally use a block of snow as a door but keep it
loose fitting and on the inside so it does not freeze
up and jam.

Igloo

An igloo takes time to construct but makes a very efficient shelter. Position it so the entrance does not point into the wind. If necessary, build a wind break. To start construction mark out a circle on the ground about 4m (13.5ft) in diameter. Dig out different levels — a higher level for sleeping and a lower (cold) level for storage — and dig an entrance tunnel. Trample down the snow to make the floor. Then cut and lay a circle of snow blocks on the perimeter of the circle. Add a layer of blocks on top, centring new blocks over vertical joints below. Build up more layers, placing each layer halfway over the lower tier, so the igloo tapers in, and seal the top with a flat block (a). Create an entrance arch using large blocks to protect the opening to the entrance tunnel (b). Make ventilation holes near the top and bottom of the igloo — avoid the side of the prevailing wind or low down where snow rapidly builds up and blocks them. Fill other gaps with snow and smooth off the inside to remove drip-points.

must know

Living in an igloo
- Check ventilation holes do not become blocked by snow or ice.
- Regularly remove snow from the entrance to maintain access.
- Mark the entrance so that it is easily found.
- Keep a supply of fuel inside the shelter.
- Knock snow off boots and clothing before entering.
- Keep shovels and tools inside so you can dig yourself out.
- Stop drips by placing a piece of snow on the source.
- Relieve yourself inside the shelter to conserve body heat. Use containers, emptying them whenever possible.

a   b

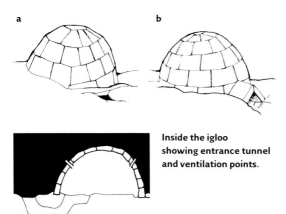

Inside the igloo showing entrance tunnel and ventilation points.

must know

Water-borne disease
Most of the common diseases
caught whilst living in harsh
conditions outdoors are water-
borne. Pollution of drinking
water must be avoided.

Camp hygiene

Strict hygiene should be practised while camping if
good health is to be maintained: make sure each
person knows the dangers of poor hygiene. Rubbish
and latrines must be kept well away from the camp
to reduce the risk of pollution of drinking water.

Rubbish disposal

Rubbish should be burned using a large can as an
incinerator. What cannot be burned should be buried.

Latrines

Latrines should be dug downhill of the camp and
away from the water supply. If a latrine starts to
smell, fill it in, burn old timbers and dig a new one.

**Deep trench latrine: Dig a
trench about 1.25m (4ft)
deep and 45cm (18in)
wide. Build up the sides
with logs or rocks and
earth to sitting height.
Lay logs across the top,
leaving a hole for use (a).
Empty wood ash on the
logs to make a seal — it
will also deter flies. Cover
the opening with a
wooden lid, flat rock or
large leaf weighted down
with stones (b).**

**Urinal: Dig a pit about
60cm (2ft) deep. Fill it
three-quarters full with
large stones and top it up
with earth. Use a bark
cone set into the pit as
a funnel.**

Drinking water

When collecting water from a stream or river, establish a point from which drinking water is to be taken and ensure that no one washes, cleans pots, scrubs clothes or otherwise uses the stream upstream of this point. If in doubt about the purity of the water, filter and boil it before drinking. To filter, allow the water to stand in a container so that sediment settles at the bottom. Then siphon it into a filter made from a nylon stocking (or other porous material) stuffed with layers of sand (at the bottom) and charcoal and moss (at the top). In emergencies use the sterilising tablets in your medical kit to make water safe to drink.

Soap

Washing with soap leaves the skin less waterproof and more prone to attack by germs. However, soap is an antiseptic and ideal for scrubbing hands before administering first aid for wounds. Save your supplies for this.

Making soap

Two ingredients — an oil and alkali — are needed to make soap. The oil can be obtained from animal fat or vegetables, but not from minerals. The alkali can be produced by burning wood or seaweed to make ash. Wash the ash with water, then strain and boil it with the oil. Simmer until the excess liquid is evaporated and allow the mixture to cool. Add horseradish root or pine resin to make the soap antiseptic. Note that too much alkali in soap dries the skin, leaving it sore.

must know

Camp discipline
- ▶ Never urinate or defecate near your water supply.
- ▶ Do not use disinfectant in a latrine. Cover faeces with earth. Make a latrine cover to keep out flies and always replace it.
- ▶ Keep food covered and off the ground.
- ▶ Replace lids on water bottles and containers immediately after use.
- ▶ Stow spare clothing and equipment in your shelter to keep it clean and dry.
- ▶ Never leave a fire unattended.

Fire

Fire can be a life saver. It provides warmth, protection and a means of signalling; it boils water, cooks and preserves food; and it can be used to scare away wild animals or keep insects at bay. Learn to light a fire anywhere under any conditions. It is not enough to know all the methods — you must be expert at them.

Preparation

Choose a sheltered site. Except for signalling purposes, do not light a fire at the base of a tree or stump. Clear away leaves, twigs, moss and dry grass from a circle at least 2m (6ft) across and scrape away everything until you have a surface of bare earth.

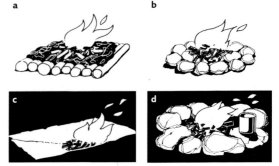

If the ground is wet, build the fire on a platform made from a layer of green logs covered with a layer of earth (a), or a layer of stones (b). In windy conditions, build the fire in a trench (c), or encircle it with rocks (d). The rocks will keep your pots warm and can be used later as bed warmers.

Tinder

Tinder is any kind of material that takes only a spark to ignite it. Keep it dry in a waterproof container. The following make good tinder: birch bark, dried grasses, fine wood shavings, bird down, waxed paper, cotton fluff from clothing, pulverised fir cones, pine needles or the inner bark from cedar trees, dried fungi (powdered), scorched or charred cotton or linen (ground finely), dust produced by wasps boring into trees, powdery bird and bat droppings, down feathers, dry fieldmouse nests.

Kindling

Kindling is the wood used to raise the flames from the tinder. Small dry twigs, resinous woods and softer woods are best. Kindling must be dry. Take it from standing deadwood rather than the damp earth. If the outside is wet or damp, shave until the dry middle is reached.

Fuel

Use dry wood to get the fire going. Once it is established you can mix in green wood, or damp wood if you want smoke to deter insects. To keep wood dry, build a basic woodshed in a place where it is warmed by the fire but clear of stray sparks.

▶ **Hardwoods:** Hickory, beech or oak burn well, are long-lasting and give off good heat.
▶ **Softwoods:** Tend to burn too fast and spark. The worst culprits are cedar, alder, hemlock, spruce, pine, chestnut and willow.

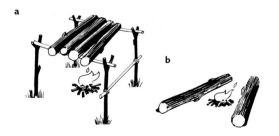

a

b

> **must know**
>
> **Exploding rocks**
> Avoid placing wet or porous rocks near fires — they may explode when heated, producing dangerous flying fragments. Test by banging rocks together: do not use any that crack or make a hollow sound.

Make fire sticks by shaving sticks with shallow cuts to 'feather' them. This helps the wood catch light more quickly.

To dry wood: Lie it across two supports at a safe distance above the fire (a). Or lay green logs at an angle beside the fire, tapering away from the wind so they shelter the fire while they dry (b).

Save energy: Instead of chopping logs, break them over a rock (a). Or feed them over the fire, letting them burn through in the middle (b). Split logs without an axe by placing a small knife on the end and hitting it with a rock (c). Plug a wooden wedge in the opened gap and drive this downward to complete the split.

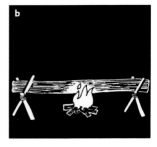

Alternative fuels

In areas where wood is difficult to find, you may need to use other fuels, some of which require special preparation.

▶ **Animal droppings:** Dry well and mix with grass, moss and leaves.

▶ **Peat:** Found on moors, it is springy underfoot and looks black and fibrous. Cut with a knife and dry before burning. Needs good ventilation when burning.

▶ **Coal:** This is sometimes found on the surface in the northern tundra.

▶ **Shales:** These are rich in oil and burn readily. Some sands also contain oil and burn with a thick smoke — useful for signalling.

▶ **Combustibles:** Petroleum, hydraulic fluid, engine oils, insect repellent. Tyres, upholstery and rubber seals are inflammable, especially when soaked in oil.

▶ **Animal fats:** Burn with a wick in a tin.

Burning oil and water

This mixture is highly volatile and makes one of the hottest of all fires. Pierce a small hole in the base of a tin can for each liquid and fit a tapered stick to govern the flow (a). To increase flow pull out the stick; push in to reduce. The oil and water run down a trough to a metal plate. Try 2–3 drops water: 1 drop oil. Light a small fire under the plate to get it hot. Then light the mixture to produce flames above the plate.

Fire lighting

To light a fire, first make a bed of tinder and form a wigwam of kindling around it (a). In windy weather, lean the kindling against a log on the lee side (b). Ignite the tinder and add larger sticks once the kindling has caught fire. Alternatively, light a bundle of dry twigs, then place them in the wigwam (c).

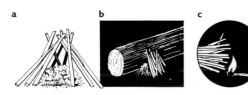

a   b   c

Matches

Matches are the easiest way to start a fire. Carry the non-safety type in waterproof containers, packed so they cannot rub together and ignite. Split matches in half to make them go further. To strike split matches, press the inflammable end against the striking surface with a finger.

Using a lens

Sunlight, focused through a lens, can produce sufficient heat to ignite tinder. Use your survival kit magnifying glass or a telescope or camera lens to focus the sun's rays. Blow on the tinder as it begins to glow.

Flint and steel

Flint is a stone found in many parts of the world. Strike the flint with a steel blade and hot sparks will fly off, which will ignite dry tinder (a). For more sparks, use the saw-edged blade from your survival kit to draw across the ridged surface of the flint supplied with it (b).

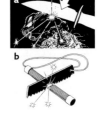

**Put a pinch of sand in the
spindle hole to increase
the friction.**

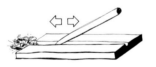

Battery fire lighting

A spark from a battery can start a fire. If using a car
battery, remove it from the vehicle first. Attach two
lengths of wire to the terminals, or use metal tools if
you have no wire. Slowly bring the bare ends of the
two pieces of wire together. A spark will jump across
before they touch. Aim it at the tinder. A small piece
of cloth with a little petrol is the best tinder for this.

Hand drill

This fire-making technique uses friction to create
heat and ignite the tinder. Cut a V-shaped notch in a
hardwood baseboard and make a small depression
near it. Use a stem of hollow softer wood with a soft
pith core for a spindle. Roll the spindle between the
palms of your hands while running your hands
downwards, pressing the spindle into the
depression. The tinder produced will ignite if you
blow gently on the spindle tip when it glows red.

Fire plough

This method of ignition also works by friction. Cut a
straight groove in a softwood baseboard and then
plough the tip of a hardwood shaft up and down it.
The action produces tinder and then ignites it.

Fires for warmth

An outdoor fire warms only the surfaces that are
facing it. For more warmth build a reflector.

**Site the fire near a rock and add a
reflector. Sit between the two so
the rock reflects the heat and
warms your back (a). If there is no
rock to reflect heat, place a
second reflector behind you (b).**

Fires for preserving meat and fish

A snake hole fire is ideal for smoke preserving or burning rubbish. To make one, dig a chamber about 45cm (18in) deep into the side of a firm earth bank. Make a chimney by driving a stick down from above into the chamber, manoeuvring it a little and removing the spoil that falls below. Build the fire inside the chamber. The entrance is best sited downwind in blustery conditions.

Fires for cooking

These cooking fires are also good for heating.

Trench fire

Positioned below ground level, a trench fire is well sheltered from strong winds. Dig a trench 30 x 90cm (12 x 36in) and 30cm (12in) deep and line the bottom with a layer of rocks. Then build a fire on the rocks. When the fire dies down, the rocks will remain hot enough to make a grill.

A spit placed across the embers is ideal for roasts.

Hobo stove

This stove provides a heat source and the top can be used for cooking. Punch holes in the base and around the bottom of the sides of a five-gallon oil drum to allow a draught to enter. Cut out a panel on one side, 5cm (2in) from the bottom, through which to stoke the fire. Set the drum on a ring of stones to allow ventilation from below.

Cooking

Whether you bring your own food or collect it from the wild, cooking will usually improve its flavour and make it easier to digest. It also destroys any bacteria and parasites that may be present, and neutralises most poisons. Use a slow burning fire of embers and hot ash for best results.

Cooking tips
► Never leave a fire unattended when cooking.
► Having lit a fire, always have water boiling (unless in short supply) for hot drinks, sterilising wounds, etc.
► Do not balance a can on the fire. Support it on rocks or suspend it over the fire.
► Boiling conserves natural juices and retains all the fat — always drink the liquid unless boiling out toxic substances.

Boiling

Tin cans and metal boxes are ideal for boiling water. Make a handle, hang the container from a pot support or use pot tongs to take it on and off the fire. If no metal containers are available, use a thick length of bamboo to hold liquid, or make a container from birch bark — but do not let it boil dry.

Roasting

Skewer the meat on a spit and turn it over hot embers or beside a blazing fire. Keep turning the meat so the fat continually moves over the surface.

A spit should be set to one side of the fire to allow space for a drip tray to catch fat for basting.

Grilling

Grilling wastes fat so use this method only when food is plentiful. Rest a wire mesh or a grid of green sticks on rocks over embers. Hot rocks beside the fire can also be used as grilling surfaces. You can barbecue meat and vegetables by skewering the food on sticks and holding it over the fire, or use a stick supported across glowing embers by a forked stick on each side.

Baking

Slow cooking on a steady heat tenderises meat and is ideal for root vegetables. Cook the meat on a dish and baste it with its own fat. Use an oven made from a large metal box with a hinged lid and a catch you can use as a handle. Set it up to open sideways, or downwards if there is no catch. When the lid is closed, avoid a tightly sealed fit, which could build up dangerous pressure inside. If no tin is available, make a clay dome, leaving a small opening which can be sealed when baking. Set a fire inside and scrape this out before you start cooking.

A metal box oven: Stand the tin on rocks so that a fire can be lit under it. Build up rocks and earth around the back, sides and top for insulation. For ventilation, leave a space behind, and make a chimney hole from above leading to this space.

Steaming

Steaming is an excellent way to cook fish and vegetables. Punch holes in a can and suspend it inside a larger can, or put stones in the larger can to keep the inner one above the water. Cover the outer can, but not so tightly that pressure builds up causing it to explode.

Frying

Frying is a good way to vary diet, if fat is available. Any sheet of metal that can be fashioned into a curve can be used for frying vegetables or meat.

Cooking in clay

No utensils are needed, and food cooked this way requires little preparation and retains good flavour. Wrap the food in a ball of clay and place it in the embers. Heat radiates through the clay, which protects the food against scorching.

Cooking techniques

Food	Technique
Meat	Cut into cubes, boil and simmer until tender. Marinate tough meat in citric juice for 24 hours before cooking.
Fish	Stew or wrap in leaves and place in hot embers (avoid toxic leaves).
Shellfish	Safest boiled as it may contain harmful organisms. All seafood spoils quickly and must be cooked as soon as possible. Drop into boiling salted water and boil for ten minutes.
Eggs	Boil or roast. If roasting, first pierce a small hole in one end using a sharp stick or knifepoint. Place on warm embers to cook slowly.
Green vegetables	Wash in clean water and boil until tender. Steam if you are sure they are safe to eat. Eat fresh greens raw as salad if you can wash them thoroughly.
Roots	Any toxins are destroyed by heat. Try boiling for five minutes then place them in a hole dug beneath the fire, cover with ash and embers and leave until tender.
Lichens and mosses	Soak overnight in clean water. Add to stews.
Nuts	Extract oil from nuts such as beech. Crack open and separate the meat from the shells. Boil gently in water, skimming off the oil as it rises to the surface.

Useful utensils

Make a set of utensils out of sticks and birch bark.

Tongs

Lash two sticks together so they spring apart at the ends — use a tapering piece of wood between them under the lashings to hold them apart. Grip is improved if one end is forked. Use for holding hot pots.

Pot rod

Drive a sturdy forked stick into the ground near the fire. Rest a longer stick across it with one end over the fire — weight down the other end with heavy rocks. Cut a groove near the tip to prevent pots from slipping off, or tie on a strong hook.

Variable pot hook

This hanging device controls the distance between the fire and the food, which affects the speed at which the food cooks. Use a strong branch with several smaller side branches. Trim the side branches to 10-12cm (4-5in). Strip off the bark.

Birch bark containers

Use the inner layer of birch bark to make cooking vessels. Secure the vessels near the top to prevent unfolding. A circle, folded into quarters, will make a cone-shaped cup or a boiling vessel if suspended.

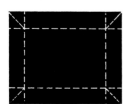

Preserving food

The deterioration of food can be delayed by keeping it in cool places such as caves or by water. For longer-term preservation you can try drying, smoking, pickling and salting. Soft fruit will keep for longer as a sugar preserve.

Drying

Wind and sun can dry food but it is easier to force-dry it over a fire. Meat with a high fat content is difficult to preserve. Cut off the fat, rub salt into the flesh and hang the salted meat in a cool airy place.

Smoke drying

This dehydrates the meat or fish and coats it with a protective layer. Use a smoke tepee. Get a fire going to produce hot embers and add green leaves to produce smoke. Leaves from hardwood trees are best. Avoid holly and other toxic leaves, and conifers which may burst into flame. Cut meat into

A smoke tepee: Build it by driving three sticks into the ground to form a triangle and tying the tops together. Make a platform between them and a fire beneath.

fat-free strips; gut and fillet fish. Cover the tepee with a cloth, or use boughs and turves to seal it. Leave the food to dry for 18 hours, making sure that the smoke does not escape. The food will dry slowly and become coated with smoke without being cooked.

Nuts and cereals
Place these on hot rocks from the fire, turning frequently until dried. Store in damp-proof containers.

Fruit, berries and fungi
These can be dried whole or cut into slices and dried by sun, smoke or heat. Fruit can be eaten dry. Add fungi to soups or soak in water for several hours to regain their texture.

Pickling and salting
Citric acid from limes and lemons can be used to pickle fish and meat. Dilute the juice with water 2:1, mix well and soak the flesh for at least 12 hours. Transfer it to an airtight container with enough solution to cover the meat. Vegetables can be preserved by pickling or by boiling and then keeping them in salt water. To make sure a brine solution is strong enough, add salt until a potato or root vegetable will float in it. Another method of using salt is to tightly pack layers of salt and vegetables, thoroughly washing off the salt when you want to use the food.

Sugar preserves
Fresh fruit can be boiled and made into jellies. Most fruit contains pectin, which reacts with acid in the fruit to form a jelly when cool. For fruits that contain less pectin, boil with crab apples or other pectin-rich fruits.

want to know more?

Take it to the next level...
► **For more on using fire for signalling** 145-7
► **For more on edible and poisonous plants and animals** 69-89
► **For more on dangerous creatures** 116-29

Other sources...
► **Learn more about knots and net-making from specialist books and courses. There is a knot for every job and it is important to select the right one for the task.**
► **For the best type of rope to take with you, and how to keep it in good condition, seek advice from climbing clubs and outdoor suppliers.**
► **Learn techniques for felling a tree from a tree surgeon or forester. They could prove useful.**

3 Water and food

Satisfying your body's nutritional requirements is vital for survival in the wild. You should know how to acquire drinking water and food in case your supplies run out. Techniques for water collection, gathering edible plants and trapping animals and fish are covered in this chapter.

Water and salt

An adult can survive for three weeks without food but only three days without water. Do not wait until you run out of water before you look for more. In hot climates you may need to replace lost salt. Learn to recognise the symptoms of salt deprivation and be ready to act quickly.

must know

How to retain fluids
To keep fluid loss to a minimum, take the following precautions:
▶ Avoid exertion.
▶ Do not smoke.
▶ Keep cool.
▶ Eat as little as possible — digestion uses up fluids, increasing dehydration. Fat is especially hard to digest.
▶ Avoid drinking alcohol. It takes fluid from vital organs to break it down.
▶ Keep healthy: vomiting and diarrhoea increase water loss.

Finding freshwater

Look in valley bottoms where water naturally drains. Take water from small river outlets — large rivers tend to be full of silt and may be polluted. If there is no stream or pool, look for patches of green vegetation and dig there.

▶ **Arid regions:** Try digging at the lowest point of the outside bend of a dry stream bed or at the lowest point between dunes.

▶ **Mountainous regions:** Look for water trapped in crevices and other rock faults.

▶ **Coastal regions:** Dig above the high water line where fresh water filters down and floats on the heavier salt water. It may be brackish but is still drinkable. Or look for lush vegetation in faults in cliffs: you may find a spring. Coastal rock pools are unlikely to be freshwater, even above the high water mark. They may be the result of wave splash. Sometimes you can identify fresh water by the presence of green algae, normally grazed by saltwater molluscs but untouched in areas of reduced salinity. Never drink sea water without distilling it first. Far from quenching your thirst, it will take valuable body fluids away from the vital organs and eventually cause the kidneys to fail.

Dew and rain collection

Collecting dew and rain is an excellent way to obtain freshwater. For rainwater collection use as large a catchment area as possible and run the water off into containers. A hole dug in the ground and lined with clay or an impermeable sheet will hold water efficiently, but keep it covered. If you have no sheeting, use bark to catch the water.

In climates where it is hot during the day and cold at night, heavy dew can be expected. It will condense on metal objects from where it can be sponged or licked off. Alternatively, use clothing to soak up water and then wring it out.

If you have any doubt about the water you have collected, boil it.

must know

Always keep a water supply
Though all water can be sterilised, you should aim to have a supply of fresh water at all times. Seek out new sources of fresh running water wherever you are.

Animals as signs of water	
Animals	**Signs**
Mammals	Grazing animals are usually never far from water as they need to drink at dawn and dusk. Converging game trails often lead to water: follow them downhill. Meat-eating animals are not good indicators of water — they get moisture from animals on which they prey and visit water sources only infrequently.
Birds	Grain eaters, such as finches and pigeons, are never far from water. They drink at dawn and dusk. When they fly straight and low they are heading for water. On their return, they are loaded with water and fly from tree to tree, resting frequently. Water birds and birds of prey are not good indicators of local water.
Reptiles	Not indicators of water.
Insects	Good indicators, especially bees, which fly at most 6.5km (4 miles) from their nests or hives, but have no regular watering times. Ants are dependent upon water. A column of ants marching up a tree is going to a small reservoir of trapped water. Most flies keep within 90m (100yds) of water.

must know

Polluted water
Be suspicious of any pool with
no green vegetation growing
around it, or animal bones
present. It is likely to be polluted.
Check edges for minerals which
may indicate alkaline conditions.
Always boil water from pools.

Condensation

Trees can draw moisture from a water table 15m
(50ft) or more below ground — too deep for you to
dig. Let the tree pump it up for you by tying a plastic
bag around a leafy branch. Evaporation from the
leaves will produce condensation in the bag.

**Keep the mouth of
the bag at the top
and a corner hanging
low to collect water.**

**Use a polythene tent to collect
moisture over vegetation.
Suspend the tent from the apex.
Collect water from plastic-lined
channels at the bottom.**

**Cut vegetation will produce condensation when placed in
a large plastic bag. Raise the foliage off the bottom with
stones so the water can collect below. Support the top on a
padded stick and keep the bag taut. Arrange the bag on a
slope so condensation runs down to a collecting point.**

**Solar still: Use a syphon to a lower
level to draw off water without
disturbing the still.**

Solar still

In climates where it is hot by day and cold at night,
try collecting condensation using a solar still. Dig a
hole in the ground 90cm (36in) across and 45cm
(18in) deep. Place a collecting can in the centre, then
cover the hole with a sheet of plastic formed into a
cone shape, with a weight in the centre. When the
sun raises the temperature of the air and soil, water
vapour is produced, which condenses during the
cold nights on the underside of the plastic and runs

down into the container. A still like this can collect 570ml (1pt) over a 24-hour period.

Distillation

If no freshwater can be found, you can obtain pure water by distilling saltwater. Pass a tube into the top of a water-filled covered container, placed over a fire, and the other end into a sealed collecting tin. The tin should be set inside another container providing a jacket of cold water to cool the vapour as it passes out of the tube. To avoid wasting water vapour, seal around the joins with wet sand.

Water from ice and snow

Ice produces twice as much water as snow for half the heat so it is better to melt ice rather than snow. If you are forced to heat snow, melt a little in a pot, then gradually add more. Filling the pot causes a hollow to form at the bottom as the snow melts, which makes the pot burn. Note that surface snow yields less water than the lower compacted layers.

Water from plants

Another way to collect freshwater is directly from plants.

Water collectors

Plants often trap water in cavities. For instance, the old, hollow joints of bamboo fill up with water. Shake them — if you hear water, cut a notch at the base of each joint and tip the water out.

Vines

Vines with rough bark and shoots about 5cm (2in) thick can be a useful source of water. (But beware:

Cup-shaped plants catch and hold water. Strain the liquid to remove insects and debris.

Coconut milk

A safe and refreshing drink, but the milk from ripe nuts is a powerful laxative: drinking too much will make you lose more fluid.

not all have drinkable water — some yield a poisonous, milky sap and others cause a skin irritation on contact.) Select a stem and trace it upwards. Reach as high as possible and cut a deep notch in the stem. Cut off the same stem close to the ground and let the water drip from it. When it ceases to drip, cut a section from the bottom and repeat until the vine is drained. Do not cut the bottom of the vine first beause it will cause the liquid to run up the vine through capillary action.

Roots

In Australia the water tree, desert oak and bloodwood have their roots near the surface. Pry the roots out from the ground and cut them into 30cm (12in) lengths. Remove the bark. Suck out the moisture, or shave to a pulp and squeeze it over your mouth.

The Saquarro cactus of Mexico and USA grows to 5m (17ft) and holds large amounts of poisonous fluid. Make it safe to drink by placing it in a solar still to evaporate and recondense overnight.

Palms

The buri, coconut and nipa palms all contain a sugary fluid which is drinkable. To start it flowing, bend a flowering stalk downwards and cut off its tip. If a thin slice is cut off the stalk every 12 hours the flow will be renewed, making it possible to collect up to 1 litre (2 pints) each day. Nipa palms shoot from the base so you can work from ground level.

Cacti

Both the fruit and bodies of cacti store water, but some cacti are very poisonous. Avoid contact with the spines, which can cause festering sores.

The barrel cactus can reach a height of 120cm (4ft) and is found in the southwestern United States through to South America. The spine-covered outer

Prickly pears have big 'ears' and produce oval fruits which ripen to red or gold. Both fruit and ears are moisture laden.

skin is tough: cut off the top and chop out pieces from the inside to suck, or smash the pulp within the plant and scoop out the watery sap, which varies from tasteless in some plants to bitter in others.

Water from animals

All fish contain a drinkable fluid. Large fish, in particular, have a reservoir of fresh water along the spine. Tap it by gutting the fish and (keeping the fish flat) removing the backbone — you can then pour off the liquid.

Desert animals can also be a source of moisture. In northwestern Australia, aborigines dig for desert frogs that burrow in the ground. Their bodies store water which can be squeezed out of them.

Animal eyes contain water. If desperate you can extract the moisture by sucking the eyes.

Salt

A normal diet includes a daily intake of 10gm (0.5oz) of salt. This is to replace salt lost in sweat and urine. The warmer the climate the greater the loss, and physical exertion increases the loss. You must replace all lost salt to maintain good health.

Obtaining salt

If you are near the coast, 0.5 litres (1 pint) of sea water contains about 15g (0.75oz) of salt, but do not drink it as it is. Dilute it with plenty of fresh water to make it drinkable, or evaporate it to get salt crystals.

Inland, salt can be obtained from plants such as the roots of hickory trees in North America or the nipa palm in southeastern Asia. Boil the roots until the water evaporates and black salt crystals are left.

The barrel cactus

A 100cm (3.5ft) barrel cactus will yield about 1 litre (2 pints) of milky juice. This is an exception to the rule to avoid milky-sapped plants for food and drink.

must know

Salt deficiency
The first symptoms are muscle cramps, dizziness, nausea and tiredness. The remedy is to take a pinch of salt in half a litre (a pint) of water. There should be salt tablets in your survival kit. Break them up and dissolve an appropriate amount in water. Do not swallow them whole as this can cause stomach upsets and kidney damage.

Food

A healthy body can survive for a time on reserves stored in its tissues, but lack of food makes it increasingly difficult to keep warm, to recover after hard work or injury and to fight off disease. When supplies run out you need to know how to maintain a balanced diet while living off the land.

good to know

Energy needs
Work or major activity can burn up over 5,500 calories daily. Simple activities such as standing up, sitting down, lighting a fire, etc, use up around 45 calories per hour. The body in a restful state requires 70 calories per hour just for breathing and basic bodily functions. If food is scarce, do not squander energy.

Balancing your diet

A balanced diet is as important as having enough to eat. It must include the right proportions of fat, protein, carbohydrates, minerals and vitamins. If carbohydrates and fats are missing, protein is used to generate energy but at the expense of the body's other needs, so that in starvation the body burns up its own tissues.

Carbohydrates

Easily digested, carbohydrates are a good source of energy and they prevent ketosis (nausea caused by excessive breakdown of body fat during starvation). They come in two forms: sugars found in sugar, syrup, honey, treacle and fruits; and starches in cereals, roots and tubers.

Fats

A concentrated source of energy, fats are digested slowly and require an adequate intake of water during the digestive process. They are found in animals, fish, eggs, milk, nuts and some vegetables and fungi.

Proteins

Also a source of energy, proteins are found in meat, fish, eggs and dairy produce, and plants in the form

Sources of energy

Fat: 1g (0.035oz) produces 9 calories.
Carbohydrate: 1g (0.035oz) produces 4 calories.
Protein: 1g (0.035oz) produces 4 calories.

of nuts, grains, pulses and fungi. Animal protein contains all the amino acids humans need, but plant foods do not unless a sufficient range is eaten.

Minerals

Calcium, phosphorus, sodium, chlorine, potassium, sulphur and magnesium are among those minerals required in quantity. Iron, fluorine and iodine are required in much smaller amounts. All have vital roles in body functions.

Trace elements

These are certain chemicals in tiny amounts. Their exact function is not yet understood.

Vitamins

About a dozen vitamins are essential for humans. Vitamin D can be synthesized by the body when exposed to sun and vitamin K by bacteria in the gut. Others must come from external sources. Beri-beri, scurvy, rickets and pellagra are all the result of vitamin deficiency. Vitamin A aids vision and prevents eye disease.

Food plants

There are few places without some kind of vegetation that can be eaten. Plants contain essential vitamins and minerals, and are rich in protein and carbohydrates. Some contain fat and all provide roughage.

Gathering plants

Gather plants systematically. Take a container on foraging trips to stop the harvest being crushed.

must know

Plants safe to eat
▶ Do not assume that because birds, mammals or insects have eaten a plant that it is safe for humans.
▶ Although one part of a plant can be eaten another may be poisonous. Test leaves, stems, roots and fruits separately (see page 70).

Edible plants

In Europe alone there are 10,000 edible wild plants. Some plants, though edible, have very little food value, so learn which yield the most nourishment and which are poisonous.

▶ **Leaves and stems:** Young growth is tastier and more tender. Older plants are tough and bitter. Nip off leaves near the stem — tearing them off may damage them.

▶ **Roots and tubers:** Choose larger plants. If difficult to pull up, dig around the plant to loosen, then prise them out with a sharpened stick.

▶ **Fruit and nuts:** Pick only ripe, fully coloured fruit. Hard, greenish berries are indigestible. Peel tough, bitter skins. Nuts lying at the base of a tree are a sign they are ready. Others can be shaken down or knocked down with a stick.

Edibility test

Adopt the following procedure when trying plants as foods. One person only should complete the full test. Never take short cuts. If in doubt at any stage, do not eat the plant.

▶ **Inspect:** Try to identify. Ensure the plant is not slimy or worm-eaten. Do not risk old, withered plants, which may have become toxic.

▶ **Smell:** Crush a small portion. If it smells of bitter almonds or peaches, discard it.

▶ **Skin irritation:** Rub some of the juice onto a tender part of your body (e.g. under the arm between armpit and elbow). If discomfort, a rash or swelling is experienced, discard it.

▶ **Lips, tongue, mouth:** If there is no irritation so far, proceed to the following stages, waiting 15 seconds between each to check there is no unpleasant reaction:
- Place a small portion on the lips
- Place a small portion in the corner of the mouth
- Place a small portion on the tip of the tongue
- Place a small portion under the tongue
- Chew a small portion

Discard the plant if any discomfort is felt, e.g. soreness to throat, irritation, stinging or burning.

▶ **Swallow:** Wait five hours after swallowing a small amount. During this period do not eat or drink anything else.

▶ **Eating:** If no adverse reactions, e.g. soreness to the mouth, belching, nausea, stomach pains, you may consider the plant safe to eat.

▶ **Seeds and grains:** Some contain deadly poisons. Taste, but do not swallow. Carry out the edibility test and reject any seed that is unpalatable, bitter or with a hot, burning taste (unless a positively identified pepper or spice).

▶ **Fungi:** Medium-sized are easier to identify. Pick the whole fungus — the stem will aid identification. Keep fungi separate as poisonous ones will contaminate other food.

▶ **Tree sap:** Tap birch or maple sap to make high-energy syrup. Cut a V-shape in the bark. Below the V make a hole, insert a leaf in the trunk as a drip spout and run the sap into a container. Collect the sap daily and boil it to produce a thick syrup.

Identifying plants

There are many plants across the world that can be used as survival foods. A selection is shown on the colour pages that follow. Use a field guide to help identify each species and to build up your knowledge of edible and poisonous plants.

Many familiar kitchen herbs grow wild. Their smells will help to identify them. Fruits and nuts growing in the wild will also be familiar from their cultivated forms.

Some roots contain toxins. If unsure of their identity, thoroughly cook to make them safe to eat.

There are no reliable rules for identifying fungi, poisonous or edible. Cooking does not destroy their poisons. The best advice is to learn to recognise a small number and stick to them, for instance the selection included in the following colour-page section. Learn also the Amanita family — they include fungi that can kill.

Plants to avoid

Plant poisons

There are two common poisons in the plant world, both easily detectable:

▶ **Hydrocyanic acid (Prussic acid):** Has the taste and smell of bitter almonds or peaches. Most notable example is the Cherry Laurel: crush the leaves and remember the smell. Discard all plants with this smell.

▶ **Oxalic acid:** The salts (oxalates) occur naturally in some plants, for instance Wild Rhubarb and Wood Sorrel. Recognisable by the sharp, dry, burning sensation when applied to the skin or tongue. Discard all plants which fit this description.

Others to avoid

▶ Any plant with a milky sap, unless positively identified as safe, e.g. dandelion.

▶ Red plants, unless positively identified.

▶ Fruit which divides into five segments, unless positively identified as safe.

▶ Grasses and other plants with tiny barbs on their stems and leaves: the hooks will irritate the mouth and digestive tract.

▶ Old or wilted leaves — some develop deadly hydrocyanic acid when they wilt, e.g. blackberry, raspberry, cherry, peach and plum. All may be eaten safely when young, fresh and dry.

▶ Mature bracken. It destroys vitamin B in the body and can cause death. Eat only tightly coiled 'fiddle heads'. All northern temperate ferns are edible when young, but some are bitter and unpalatable and some have hairy barbs which must be removed before eating (break off young tips, close your hand over the stalk and draw the frond through to remove the 'wool').

Poisonous grains

The heads of some grain plants may have black spurs in place of normal seeds. These carry a potentially lethal poisonous, hallucinogenic fungal disease. Reject the whole head.

Food poisoning

Should stomach trouble occur, drink plenty of hot water and do not eat again until the pain goes. If severe, induce vomiting by tickling the back of the throat. Swallowing some charcoal will induce vomiting and the charcoal may absorb poison at the same time. White wood ash mixed to a paste with water will relieve stomach pain.

Temperate zone: Edible plants

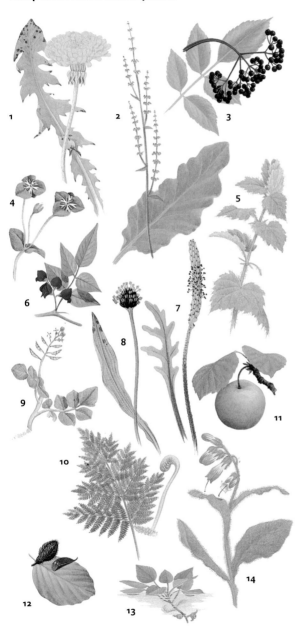

1 Dandelion:
Eat young leaves raw; boil older ones, changing water to remove bitter taste. Boil roots or roast for coffee.

2 Curled Dock:
Boil tender leaves from young plants, changing water to remove bitterness.

3 European Elder:
Purplish-black berries best cooked down to a syrup. Red berries may be toxic.

4 Chickweed:
Boil tender leaves.

5 Stinging Nettle:
Boil young growth for minimum of six minutes to destroy formic acid in hairs.

6 Groundnut:
Peel tubers then roast or boil.

7 Buck's-horn Plantain:
Prepare as Plantain.

8 Plantain:
Prepare young leaves like spinach.

9 Watercress:
Leaves and stems are edible raw.

10 Bracken:
Eat only young shoots, drawing off woolly barbs and boiling for half an hour. Roots are edible boiled or roasted.

11 Crab Apple:
Best cooked with other fruit.

12 Beech:
Nuts are edible raw, roasted or crushed for oil.

13 Water Chestnut:
Seeds are edible raw or roasted.

14 Comfrey:
Roots are edible raw or cooked. Do not confuse with Foxglove.

Temperate zone: Poisonous plants

Contact poisons:
Contact produces severe irritation and rashes. Wash affected parts immediately.
1 Poison Sumac
2 Poison Oak
3 Poison Ivy
4 Jewelweed
Poisons by ingestion:
In some cases, one mouthful can kill.
5 Death Carnas
(do not confuse with Wild Onions or Lilies)
6 Thorn-apple
or Crimson Weed
7 Foxgloves
8 Monk's-hood
9 Hemlock
10 Water Hemlock or
Cowbane
11 Baneberries
12 Deadly Nightshade

Learn to recognise other common poisonous plants in addition to those illustrated, including Buttercups, Lupins, Vetches or Locoweeds, False Helleborines, Henbane. These have poisonous berries: Canadian Moonseed, Nightshades, Virginia Creeper, Buckthorns. Poisonous trees include: Yew, Cedar, Horse Chestnut and Buckeye, Laburnum, Black Locust, California Laurel or Oregon Myrtle, Moosewood or Moosebark, Hickory.

Arctic and Northern zone: Edible plants

1 Red Spruce:
Young shoots are edible raw or cooked: infuse the needles for teas and boil the edible inner bark.

2 Black Spruce:
Use as Red Spruce.

3 Labrador Tea:
Infuse leaves for tea.

4 Arctic Willow:
Spring shoots, leaves, inner bark and young peeled roots are all edible. High in vitamin C.

5 Fern:
Eat only young fiddleheads up to 15cm (6in): remove hairs, steam to cook.

6 Cloudberry:
Eat raw.

7 Salmonberry:
Eat raw.

8 Bearberry:
Cook.

9 Rock Tripe (Lichen):
Very nutritious. Soak for several hours then boil.

10 Reindeer Moss:
Soak for several hours then boil.

11 Iceland Moss:
Soak for several hours then boil.

In addition to the hardy arctic plants shown here, many temperate species occur in summer in the far north. See the selection of edible and poisonous plants on the previous pages.

Desert zone: Edible plants

1 Barrel Cactus:
An exception to the rule to avoid milky sap. Slice off the top and smash the inner pulp, then drink.

2 Prickly Pears:
Eat peeled fruit raw. Peel and cook tender young pads — cutting away the spines. Roast seeds for flour. Tap stems for water.

3 Carrion Flowers:
Tap stems for water.

4 Mescals:
Stalks not yet in flower are edible cooked.

5 Wild Gourds:
Boil unripe fruit, roast the seeds, cook young leaves. Flowers may be eaten raw, and stems and shoots chewed for water.

6 Date Palms:
Fruit and growing tip can be eaten raw; young leaves are edible cooked. Sap from trunk can be boiled down.

7 Baobabs:
Tap roots for water; eat fruits and seeds raw; boil tender young leaves.

8 Acacias:
Tap roots for water; roast seeds; boil young leaves and shoots.

9 Carob:
Pulp from seed pods can be eaten raw; hard brown seeds can be ground and then cooked as a type of porridge.

Note that some cacti are very poisonous, e.g. the Saquarro cactus contains poisonous fluid (see page 66).

Tropical zone: Edible plants

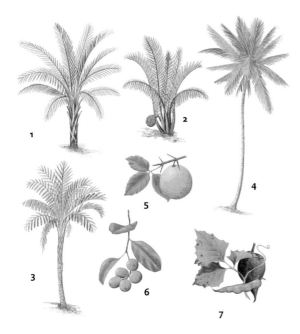

1 Sago Palm:
Spongy inner pith of trunk provides sago.
2 Nipa Palm:
Yields sugary sap, delicious fruit and edible growing tip.
3 Sugar Palm:
Collect sap and boil to a thick syrup.
4 Coconut Palm:
Growing tip, milk and flesh of nut are edible. Sap can be boiled for sugar.
5 Bael Fruit:
Fruit is edible raw and rich in vitamin C.
6 Wild Figs:
Eat fruit raw.
7 Yam Bean:
Edible tubers are crisp, sweet and juicy. Seeds must be boiled.

Many other tropical edible plants will be recognisable from their similar cultivated varieties, such as the Avocado and the whole family of citrus fruits.

Tropical zone: Poisonous plants

1 Pangi:
All parts are poisonous, especially the fruit.
2 Physic Nut:
Seed oil is violently purgative; remains of pressed seeds are very poisonous.
3 Strychnine:
Seeds of orange-like fruit are deadly poisonous.
4 Duchesnia:
Red strawberry-like fruit is highly poisonous, sometimes fatal.
**5 Castor Oil Plant
or Castor Bean:**
Seeds are violently purgative, sometimes fatally.

Among others to avoid are:
White Mangrove, Nettle Tree, Cowhage, Renghas Tree, Beachapple, Sandbox Tree.

Coastal zone: Edible plants

1 Sea Beet:
Eat leaves raw or boiled.
2 Sea Rocket:
Peppery leaves and young pods
can be eaten raw or as a potherb.
3 Sea Kale:
Tough leaves are better cooked;
slice and boil underground stems.
4 Sea Holly:
Dig out long roots, slice, boil.
5 Oyster Plant:
Leaves are edible raw or cooked.
6 Scots Lovage:
Raw leaves are rich in vitamin C.

Edible seaweeds and algae

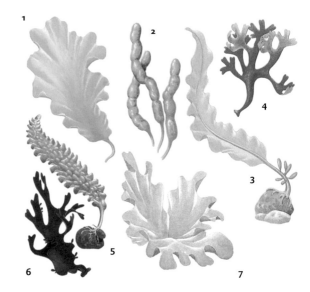

There are no poisonous
seaweeds but some irritate the
digestive tract and some are
violent purgatives.
1 Sea Lettuce:
Wash and boil.
2 Enteromorpha intestinalis:
Whole plant is edible, either
fresh or dried and pulverised.
3 Kelps:
Edible raw; better boiled.
4 Irish Moss:
Wash and boil. Fronds may be
dried for storage.
5 Sugarwrack:
Young fronds are edible raw;
better cooked.
6 Dulse:
Wash and boil.
7 Lavers:
Boil until tender, then mash.
Very tasty.

Edible fungi

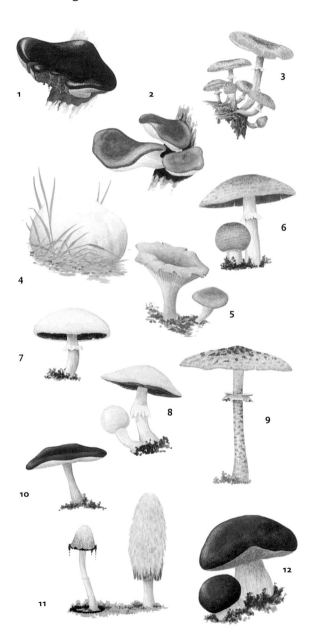

Tree fungi

1 Fistulina hepatica
(Beefsteak Fungus): Tough and bitter; young specimens are better. Soak to soften and stew thoroughly.

2 Pleurotus ostreatus
(Oyster Fungus): Tasty; slice and stew. Also dries well.

3 Armillaria mellea
(Honey Fungus): Slice and stew.

Ground fungi

4 Lycoperdon giantea
(Giant Puffball): Very tasty; simmer or fry.

5 Cantharellus cibarius
(Chanterelle): Very tasty; stew for ten minutes. Do not confuse with *Cortinarius speciosissimus* (see page 80).

6 Agaricus augustus:
Tasty; smells of anise.

7 Agaricus campestris
(Field Mushroom): Eat raw or cooked.

8 Agaricus sylvestris
(Wood Mushroom): Eat raw or cooked.

9 Lepiota procera
(Parasol Mushroom): Tastes of almonds.

10 Tricholoma nudum
(Wood Blewit or Blue Cap): Tasty and sweet-smelling. Produces an allergic reaction in a few people.

11 Coprinus comatus
(Shaggy Ink Cap): Gather young ones whose gills are still pale. Poisonous if eaten with alcohol.

12 Boletus edulis
(Cep): Many edible species. They dry well. Avoid any with pink or red spores unless positively identified. Some are poisonous.

Poisonous fungi

These are among the worst of the poisonous fungi but there are many others to avoid. Some Amanita fungi are the most deadly of all. They have a volva (cup-like appendage at the base of the stem).

1 Amanita virosa
(Destroying Angel): Sweet- and sickly-smelling and deadly poisonous. Young ones may resemble young Agaricus fungi.

2 Amanita phalloides
(Death Cap): The most deadly of all.

3 Amanita pantherina
(Panther Cap): Often fatal.

4 Amanita muscaria
(Fly Agaric): Has a distinctive bright red cap, flecked with white.

5 Entoloma sinnuatum
(Leaden Entoloma): Poisonous, can be deadly. Warning: confusable with Agaricus.

6 Inocybe patouillardii:
When young, confusable with Agaricus. Deadly poisonous.

7 Paxilus involutus:
Deadly. Do not confuse with edible yellowish fungi such as the Chanterelle.

8 Cortinarius speciosissimus:
Deadly. Do not confuse with the Chanterelle.

9 Agaricus xanthoderma
(Yellow Staining Mushroom): Poisonous and smells of carbolic. Shows a yellow stain when bruised. Do not confuse with edible Agaricus species.

Animals for food

Trapping and hunting small or larger animals for food are skills that may prove useful to have, especially in a survival situation where humane instincts must be balanced against the expediences of survival. Hunting or trapping is almost always more sussessful if you know the habits of the species you are trying to catch. Find out about animals in the area you are visiting: where they sleep, what they eat and where they water.

Mammals

Only large, powerful mammals venture out by day. Most small mammals eat at night. Learn their signs and tracks if you intend to hunt or trap them, or to avoid confrontations.

Tracking

The clearer the track the more likely it is to be recent. If dew and spiders' webs have been disturbed, the tracks are fresh. Some animals, such as rabbits, never range far and tracks will indicate they are in the area.

The height of broken twigs along a track suggest an animal's size. Droppings indicate the type of animal that left them. Check any discarded food and droppings to find out what the animal normally eats and bait traps using the same food. Other ways to locate animals include looking for recently dug earth, which may be caused by animals rooting for insects and tubers. Tracks and droppings may reveal the location of burrows and dens.

Mammal tracks and signs

Note: Tracks are not to scale. Most are typical of a whole family of animals but will vary greatly in size according to species. Track 1 is right front. Track 2 is right hind.

Wild cats (from domestic-sized wild cats to tigers)
▶ *Tracks:* Walk on toes, claws retracted when walking (except Cheetah). *Droppings:* Elongated, tapering, often hidden. Strong smelling urine.

Wild dogs (foxes, wolves, etc)
▶ *Tracks:* Walk on toes. Print shows claw tips. *Droppings:* Elongated, tapering, show remains of fur, bones, insects depending on diet. Fox droppings are pungent.

Bears
▶ *Tracks:* Prints may be 30 x 18cm (12 x 9in). Bears eat almost anything and grub up ground, rip up stumps and break into insect nests in search of food.

Otters
▶ *Tracks:* Webbed prints, almost circular 7·5 x 6cm (3 x 2.6in). *Droppings:* Fishy-smelling, elongated.

Weasel group (weasels, stoats, mink, martens, polecats)
▶ *Tracks:* Indistinct except in soft ground; often smudged by hair on main pad. Fore and rear prints overlap. Weasel tracks are the smallest.

Badgers
▶ *Tracks:* Prominent claws and large rear pad: could be confused with small bear. Stride length averages 50cm (20in). *Droppings:* Like dog's but in shallow excavated scoop. *Signs:* Disturbed ground and insect nests may indicate badgers.

Seals
▶ *Tracks:* Show belly drag in centre. Arrow indicates direction of travel.

Cattle
▶ *Tracks:* Heavy; two distinct hoofmarks, narrow at top, bulbous at rear. *Droppings:* Like familiar cowpats — they make excellent fuel when dry.

Wild sheep and goats
▶ *Tracks:* Cloven hooves, two slender pointed marks not joined, tip splayed in sheep, sometimes in goats. *Illustration:* Domestic sheep (left), chamois (right). *Droppings:* Globular, like domestic sheep.

Deer and antelopes
▶ *Tracks:* Cloven hooves form two oblongs. Reindeer marks are rounded. *Illustration:* Roe deer front and hind track (top); reindeer (bottom). Note dew-claw impressions on reindeer track. *Droppings:* Oblong to round pellets, usually in clumps. *Signs:* Scrapes on saplings, nibbled and frayed bark, long scratches where antlers have rubbed.

Wild pigs
▶ *Tracks:* Cloven hooves leave deer-like marks. On soft ground the short side toes distinguish them. *Droppings:* Often shapeless, never long, firm or tapering. *Signs:* Disturbed ground caused by rooting and mudwallows.

Rabbits and hares
▶ *Tracks:* Hairy soles leave little detail on soft ground but the combination of long hind and shorter front feet is distinctive. Hares have five toes on front feet, but inner is short and seldom leaves print. Hind foot narrower, four-toed. Rabbit similar but smaller. *Droppings:* Small, hard, round pellets. *Signs:* Bark nibbled at bottom of trees leaving two incisor marks. Rabbits thump a warning sounding like someone hitting a cushion.

Beavers
▶ *Tracks:* Five toes with claw marks, often only four show. Rear track webbed, roundish, larger 15 x 10cm (6 x 4in). *Signs:* Dam building and lodges, felled and chewed saplings, bark and shavings near water.

Hedgehogs
▶ *Tracks:* Five toes with long claws but usually only four show.

Squirrels
▶ *Tracks:* Four slender toes, with claws on front foot, five on rear. *Signs:* Chewed bark, gnawed nuts, cones beneath tree or an untidy nest of twigs in a fork.

Opossums
▶ *Tracks:* Long, spreading toes with clear claw marks.

Raccoons
▶ *Tracks:* Five long toes with clear claw marks; front foot is small and rounded, the rear is larger and tapering.

Trapping

It is easier to trap than to hunt small prey. Your choice of bait and site is important. Set traps on game trails or runs. Look for natural bottlenecks, for instance where the track passes under an obstruction. You must inspect traps regularly. Leaving a trap line unchecked will prolong an animal's pain and increase the risk of your catch being poached by predators. Choose bait from the local environment that is known to be part of the animal's diet.

A snare is the simplest of traps and should be part of any survival kit. It can be used to catch small game around the throat and larger game around the legs. The free-running noose is made of non-ferrous wire, string or rope, with a running eye at one end through which the other end passes before being firmly anchored to a stake, rock or tree.

A wire snare can be supported off the ground on twigs.

Rules for traps

When setting traps:
1 Avoid disturbing the environment: Do not leave any sign that you have been there.
2 Hide scent: When constructing or handling traps do not leave your scent on them. Wear gloves if you can.
3 Camouflage: Hide freshly cut ends of wood with mud. Use natural materials to cover a snare on the ground so that it blends in with its surroundings.
4 Make them strong: An ensnared animal will fight for its life.

Other animals for food

Do not rely only on rabbits or other obvious mammals for food. Try also:

▶ Rodents

▶ Turtles and tortoises

▶ Snakes (but do not try to catch highly poisonous or very large varieties)

▶ Frogs

▶ Insects (e.g. beetle grubs, locusts, grasshoppers, crickets, ants and termites, bees)

▶ Snails, slugs and worms

▶ Birds, especially game birds (e.g. pheasants, grouse, partridges, quail, ducks, geese, jungle fowl)

Preparing meat

First suspend the carcass head down and bleed the animal by cutting the jugular vein in its neck or the throat from ear to ear.

To skin a small mammal such as a rabbit, make an incision over the stomach (being careful not to cut into the organs), insert your thumbs and pull

Survival food

▶ **Insects:** Rich in fat, protein and carbohydrates and likely to be the most reliable source of food in a survival situation. Beware brightly coloured insects — they are usually poisonous. Avoid grubs on the underside of leaves — they often secrete poisonous fluids. Do not gather insects feeding on carrion, refuse or dung — they may carry infection. Remove legs and wings from larger insects, and the sting from bees. Smaller insects can be mashed to a paste and then either boiled, roasted or dried to a powder. Ants must be cooked for at least six minutes to destroy any poisonous formic acid.

▶ **Worms:** Contain the highest class of protein with a large proportion of essential amino acids. Starve them for a day before eating, or squeeze them to clear out muck. They can be sun- or force-dried, then ground into a powder and added to other food.

good to know

Bleeding
It is important to thoroughly bleed pigs. If blood remains in their tissues, it will speed deterioration of the flesh.

Removing the gut: the initial incision.

outwards. The skin should come away easily. Free the legs and twist the head off. With the carcass still suspended, remove the gut and recover the offal as follows: Pinch the abdomen as high as possible and in the pouch of raised flesh make a slit big enough for two fingers (do not cut through to the internal organs). Insert your fingers and use them to guide the knife as you cut upwards towards the anus and then downwards to the breastbone. Let the gut spill out. Remove the two kidneys and liver. Cut through the chest cavity membrane and remove heart, lungs and windpipe. Ensure the anus is clear. Leave the carcass hanging for 2-3 days. In hot climates, preserve the meat or cook straight away.

Fish and fishing

Fish contain protein, vitamins and fats. All freshwater fish are edible but some tropical ones can be dangerous: avoid electric eels, freshwater stingrays and the piranha of South American rivers. Angling is the most effective method of catching fish. Study their feeding habits and use appropriate bait.

Where to fish

On hot days, fish retreat to deep, shaded waters. In cold weather, they seek shallow spots where the sun warms the water. Fish like to shelter under banks and rocks. When a river is in flood, fish in slack water, for example on the outside of a bend or in a small tributary.

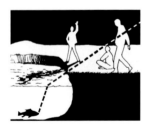

Image refraction: Fish can see more on the bank than you think. Sit or kneel when fishing, so you are less visible. Stay back from the edge and try to keep your shadow off the water.

When to fish

Leave lines out overnight and check them just before first light. If a storm is imminent, fish before it breaks. Fishing is poor after heavy rain.

Indications of fish feeding

Fish are likely to take a bait when they are feeding. Indications of feeding include fish jumping out of the water and clear ring ripples breaking on the surface. Little fish darting about may indicate pursuit by a larger predatory fish.

Angling

A fish hook and line are part of your survival kit, but you can improvise hooks from all kinds of materials. Here (in clockwise rotation) are a safety pin, a thorn, a bunch of thorns, a splinter of wood, a bone and a nail. A rod is not essential — you can fish with a handline — but it makes it easier to land fish and cast away from the bank.

Using floats and weights

▶ A small floating object attached to the line, visible from the bank, will indicate when you have a bite. Its position will help control where the line descends.

▶ Small weights between float and hook will stop the line from trailing along the water or too near the surface. Use small split lead shot from your survival kit.

▶ To get a deeper hook position, extend the line to a weight below the hook.

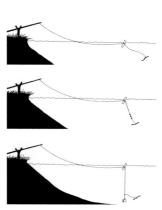

Knots for securing improvised hooks

▶ **Hook with eye:** Thread the gut. Make two turns around the hook and bring the live end up through the turns. Ease tight and test for strength.

▶ **Hook without eye:** Make a loop around the lower part of the shaft. Make two half-hitches (see page 40) from upper end downwards and pass the live end through the lower loop. Pull on the standing end to tighten.

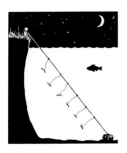

Night lines: Weight one end of a line and attach worm-baited hooks at intervals. Anchor free end securely on bank. Put this out overnight.

Bait

Bait taken from the local environment is the most effective, for example berries overhanging the water and insects breeding nearby. Scavenger fish will take pieces of meat, raw fish, ants and other insects. Once you have a catch, examine the stomach contents of the fish and replicate in bait to attract similar fish.

▶ **Ground bait:** To draw fish to the area, scatter bait on the water. A termites' or ants' nest suspended over a river is an excellent method: the fish take the insects as they fall into the river. Bait your hook with the same insects to catch the fish.

▶ **Live bait:** Worms, maggots, insects and small fish can be used. Cover the hook completely with the bait. Secure the bait without killing it, for example place the hook through the meaty part of a small fish, or through the body of a grasshopper. Its distressed movements in the water will attract fish.

▶ **Artificial bait:** Feathers tied to a hook can simulate a fly, or carve a small jointed fish out of wood (hazel is best), thread the segments and decorate with colour.

▶ **Spinning bait:** Fish will attack a shiny object drawn through the water. Try coins, buttons, pieces of tin can or buckles. Or thread a propeller shape onto a piece of wire and it will spin with the current.

Fish traps

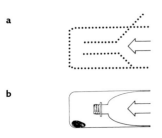

In shallow streams you can build a channel of sticks or rocks that fish swim into but are unable to turn around in (a). (The arrows indicate the current.) Another fish trap uses a bottle. Cut a plastic bottle off just below the neck. Invert the neck inside the bottle. Use bait to entice fish in (b).

a

b

If you have a net, set floats at the top and weight the bottom, then stretch the net across the river. It will soon empty a stretch of water of fish, so use only in a survival situation, and not for long.

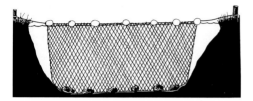

A bag is the best way to trap eels. Tie fresh offal and straw or bracken in a cloth bag. Attach a line and weight to the end of the bag and allow it to sink. Leave overnight. Eels will chew their way into the bag and will still be wriggling in the straw when you land it.

Preparing fish

Fish under 5cm (2in) long need no preparation: eat them whole. Larger fish must be gutted. As soon as the fish is caught, cut its throat to bleed it and remove the gills. To gut, make an incision from the anal orifice to the throat. Remove all offal (use it for hook bait). Keep the roe, which is very nutritious. Scaling is not necessary, but to scrape scales off, draw a knife from tail to head (a). To skin eels and catfish, pass a stake through the fish, lodge it across two uprights and cut the skin away, drawing it down towards the tail (b).

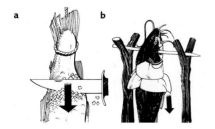

a   b

want to know more?

Take it to the next level...
▶ **For more on cooking food** 54-7
▶ **For more on how to avoid confrontations with dangerous animals** 116-29
▶ **For more on treating bites** 185-6
▶ **For more on treating poisoning** 188-9

Other sources...
▶ Extend your knowledge of plants and trees both edible and poisonous by investing in a detailed colour field guide.
▶ Refer to specialist books for guidance on hunting and trapping animals, and preparing and cooking different kinds of meat and fish.
▶ Join an angling club and practise fishing techniques before you go away.

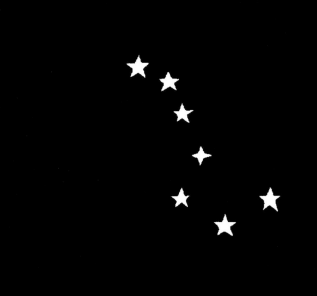

4 On the move

An ability to read a map is one of the many skills you will need when travelling across country. This chapter explains how to interpret maps and natural signs to help find your way. There are tips for predicting a change in the weather and techniques for negotiating difficult terrain.

Maps

Choose maps carefully. A large-scale map showing every footpath and building will be of no use if you are driving a thousand miles along a network of roads. On the other hand, few motoring maps give enough information about the nature of the terrain to help a walker or climber.

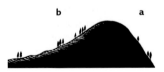

The closer the contours, the steeper the slope (a). Greater spaces between contour lines show gentler inclines (b).

Interpreting maps
Make sure you understand all the information given on your maps.

Altitude
This is recorded on maps as contour lines, representing a series of points on the ground sharing the same height above sea level.

Scale and key
Typically, a walker's map has a scale of 1:50,000, which means that each measure on the map represents a distance 50,000 times greater on the ground. Study the key and master the way information is presented: which symbols represent which features (swamps, woodlands, buildings).

Grids and coordinates
Map grids are based either on degrees of latitude and longitude or on ground measurements. You can report your location on the ground in terms of a map coordinate made up from the line references from two adjoining sides of the map. For anyone using a map with the same grid, this will immediately identify the 'box' representing the area in which you

are located. Dividing the square by eye into further tenths pinpoints your location.

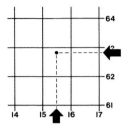

The point marked with a dot can be described as **15.5 x 62.8** using the coordinates from the grid. This system involves dividing the squares into tenths in each direction. The map coordinate is normally expressed as six digits: **155628**. Any letter area codes on the map should be included.

North on maps

Unless they are lines of longitude, grid lines do not indicate north and south, though they may be close to it. Remember that a compass points not to true north but to magnetic north — the difference between the two varies according to where you are. To take accurate bearings you need to know these local variations, but a rough idea of orientation will help you to match your map to the landscape.

Gradients

Map contours indicate the shape of the land.

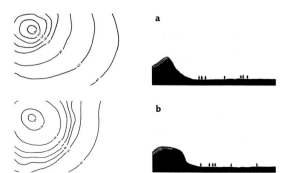

a

b

A concave slope (a), where you can see the top from the bottom of the slope, has the higher contours close together.
A convex slope (b), where you cannot see the top from the bottom, has the lower contours close together.

Direction finding

Always check your compass readings against natural indicators. You should also know how to improvise a compass in case yours is lost or broken.

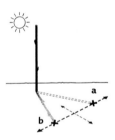

Shadow stick method 1

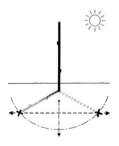

Shadow stick method 2

Direction by shadows

Shadows can be a guide to both direction and time of day. Try the following two methods for checking direction from the shadow of a stick.

Shadow method 1

On a patch of flat ground place an upright metre-long (3ft) stick. Note where its shadow falls and mark the tip with a pebble or stick (a). Wait at least 15 minutes and mark the new shadow tip (b). Join the two to show the directions of east and west — the first mark is west. North-south are at right angles to this line. This method works at any time of day and at any latitude. Use it for spot checks as you proceed.

Shadow method 2

A more accurate method is to mark the first shadow tip in the morning. Draw a clean arc at exactly this distance from the stick, using the stick as a centre point. As midday approaches the shadow will shrink and move. In the afternoon, as the shadow lengthens again, mark the spot where it touches the arc. Join the two points to give east and west — west is the morning mark.

Direction by watch

An analogue watch with two hands can be used to find direction, provided it is set to true local time (without variation for summer daylight saving and ignoring conventional time zones which do not match real time). The nearer the Equator you are, the less accurate this method will be, because it is very difficult to determine the sun's direction when it is almost directly overhead.

Watch method: northern hemisphere
Hold the watch horizontal. Point the hour hand at the sun. Bisect the angle between the hour hand and the 12 mark to give a north-south line.

Watch method: southern hemisphere
Hold the watch horizontal. Point 12 towards the sun. A mid-point between 12 and the hour hand will give you the north-south line.

Improvised compass
If you do not have a compass, make your own. Use other methods to establish the direction of north and then identify which end of your new compass needle points in this direction and mark it as north.

Suspended needle
A piece of ferrous metal wire — a sewing needle is ideal — stroked repeatedly in one direction against silk (a) will become magnetised and can be suspended so that it points north. The magnetism will be weak and will need regular topping up.

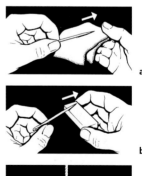

Stroking with a magnet is more efficient than using silk — stroke the metal smoothly from one end to the other in one direction only (b).

Suspend the needle in a loop of thread so balance is not affected (c). Avoid twisting the thread.

Floating needle

A better method is to lay the magnetised needle on a piece of paper, bark or grass and float it on water. Do this in camp or when making a halt.

Using electricity

If you have a power source of two volts or more (e.g. a small dry battery) the current can be used to magnetise the metal needle. You will also need a short length of wire, preferably insulated.

Coil the wire around the needle. If the wire has no insulation, wrap paper or a piece of cardboard around the needle first. Attach the ends of the wire to the terminals of the battery for five minutes.

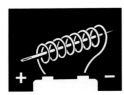

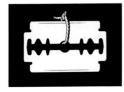

Razor blade compass

A razor blade can also be used as a compass needle. Magnetise simply by carefully stropping it against the palm of your hand.

Plant pointers

Even without a compass or the sun to give direction you can get an indication of north and south from the way a plant grows. Plants tend to grow towards the sun so their flowers and abundant growth will be to the south in the northern hemisphere, the north in the southern. Moss on tree trunks will be greener and more profuse on the sunny side. If trees have been felled, the pattern of the rings is more widely spaced on the side towards the Equator. There are even species of plant known for their north–south orientation. The North Pole Plant (a), which grows in South Africa, leans towards the north. The Compass Plant (b) of North America directs its leaves in a

a

b

north-south alignment so that its profile from east or west is quite different from that of north or south.

Prevailing winds

If the direction of the prevailing wind is known it can be used to maintain direction, but note that some wind patterns are not the same the whole year round. Where a strong wind always comes from the same direction, plants and trees may be bent that way. Birds and insects will usually build their nests in the lee of any cover, and spiders cannot spin their webs in the wind. Snow and sand dunes are also blown into distinctive patterns by a prevailing wind.

Direction by the heavens

The moon and the stars can be used to navigate.

Using the moon

If the moon rises before the sun has set, the illuminated side will be on the west. If the moon rises after midnight, the illuminated side will be in the east. This gives you a rough east-west reference during the night.

Illumination of the moon

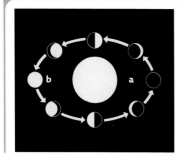

The moon has no light of its own: it reflects sunlight. As the moon orbits the earth over 28 days, the shape of the light reflected varies according to its position. When the moon is on the same side of the earth as the sun, no light is reflected from the sun (a): this is the new moon. Then it reflects light on its apparent right-hand side, from a gradually increasing area as it waxes. At the full moon it is on the opposite side of the earth from the sun (b). Then it wanes, the reflecting area gradually reducing to a narrow sliver on the apparent left-hand side.

4 On the move

The Pole Star can be pinpointed in the night sky by observing constellations that circle it: the Plough, Cassiopeia and Orion. It can be used to check the variation between true (polar) north and magnetic north indicated by your compass. Point the compass at the Pole Star and note the difference between the pointer and polar north indicated by the star.

Using the stars

In the northern hemisphere groups of stars remain visible throughout the night, wheeling around the only star that does not appear to move: the Pole Star, a useful navigation aid, located almost above polar north.

The northern sky

The main constellations are the Plough or Big Dipper (a), Cassiopeia (b) and Orion (c). All circle the Pole Star (d), but the first two are recognisable groups that do not set. Use the constellations to check the position of the Pole Star as follows:

▶ Of the seven stars which form the Plough (a), the two lowest ones point to the Pole Star, about four times further away than the distance between them.

▶ A line can be drawn connecting the Plough and Cassiopeia (b) through the Pole Star. Cassiopeia is W-shaped, on the opposite side of the Pole Star and the same distance away as the Plough. On clear, dark nights this constellation overlays the Milky Way, which stretches right across the sky, appearing as a hazy band of millions of stars. The centre star of Cassiopeia points towards the Plough.

▶ Orion (c) rises above the Equator and can be seen in both hemispheres. It rises on its side, due east, and sets due west. It is further from the Pole Star than Cassiopeia and the Plough.

The southern sky

There is no equivalent of the Pole Star near the South Celestial Pole, but the Southern Cross, a constellation of five stars, can be used to locate south. To find the Southern Cross, look along the Milky Way; in the middle there is a dark patch (the

The northern sky

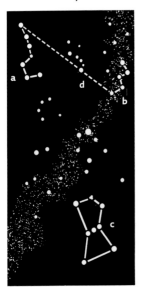

Coal Sack), and to one side of this is the Southern Cross. On the other side are two pointer stars.

The Southern Cross

Locating south

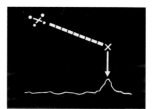

To locate south, project an imaginary line along the Southern Cross and four-and-a-half times longer, then drop it vertically down. The point where it cuts the horizon marks the direction of south — fix it using a prominent landmark, or drive two sticks into the ground to help you find it by day.

Stars that rise and set

Direction can also be determined by stars that rise and set. Set two stakes in the ground, one shorter than the other, so that you can sight along them. Look along them at any star (except the Pole Star) and it will appear to move. From the star's apparent movement you can deduce the direction in which you are facing:

Apparently rising = facing east
Apparently falling = facing west
Looping flatly to the right = facing south
Looping flatly to the left = facing north
These are only approximate directions. They are reversed in the southern hemisphere.

Passage of the stars

The stars stay in the same relation to one another and pass over the same places on the earth night after night. Their passage over the horizon starts four minutes earlier each night — a two-hour difference over a month. If you study a star at a certain position at a particular time one evening, then check its position the next evening at the same time, you will find it has moved one degree of arc anticlockwise in the northern hemisphere, clockwise in the southern. Rising in the east, stars attain a zenith and set on the western horizon at the same distance from their zenith as they rose.

Weather signs

Observing the weather can provide useful information about your local environment, and understanding weather signs will help you predict weather changes. Always aim to travel when the weather is settled.

Coastal areas

A regular pattern of day-night change in wind direction suggests a nearby large body of water — an ocean, inland sea or a lake. In these areas, breezes usually blow from sea to land during the day and off the land at night.

Winds

Certain scents — the smell of the sea or of vegetation — carried on the wind can provide information about the place from which they blow. The wind is also a guide for weather prediction, and studying the relationship between wind and different weather patterns is time well spent.

▶ If a wind is strong and dry the weather should remain constant until the wind drops or veers. Then it may rain.

▶ If it is foggy and misty you may get condensation but it should not rain — unless the wind rises and blows away the fog, in which case it may turn to rain.

Temperature difference

Water absorbs and loses heat less rapidly than the land and consequently coastal zones tend to be cooler than inland areas during the day and warmer at night.

▶ On a fine day a noticeable increase in the strength of the wind indicates an imminent weather change.

Clouds

Clouds are the most reliable of weather signs. The ten main types of cloud formation are illustrated below and on the next page.

Cirrocumulus clouds:
Look like rippled sand. An omen of fair weather, they usually follow a storm and dissipate to leave a brilliant blue sky.

Altocumulus clouds:
Fair-weather clouds, on a larger scale than cirrocumulus, thicker, not so white and with shadows in them. They usually appear after a storm.

Cumulonimbus clouds:
Low thunder clouds. Dark and menacing, they may tower to 6,000m (20,000ft), with a top flattening out into an anvil shape. They usually bring hail, a strong wind, thunder and lightning. False cirrus, very dense grey cloud, often appears above them.

Cumulus clouds:
Easily recognisable fluffy white clouds. They are usually an indication of fair weather when widely separated. If large and many-headed, they are capable of producing sudden heavy showers. Cumulus clouds at sea in an otherwise cloudless sky are often an indication of land beneath them.

Cirrus clouds:
High, wispy clouds formed from ice crystals which give them a white appearance. Often called 'mares tails', they are seen in fine weather.

Cirrostratus clouds:
Made up of ice particles and look like white veins. These are the only clouds which produce a halo around the sun or moon. If they get bigger it means fine weather, smaller a sign of rain. If a cirrus-filled sky darkens and the clouds change to cirrostratus it is an indication that rain or snow is coming.

Altostratus clouds:
Form a greyish veil through which the sun or moon may appear as a watery disk. If wet weather is approaching the cloud will thicken and darken, obscuring the sun or moon until it begins to rain.

Nimbostratus clouds:
Form low, dark blankets of cloud, which signal rain or snow within four or five hours. Usually the rain continues for hours.

Stratocumulus clouds:
Form a low, lumpy, rolling mass, usually covering the whole sky, though often thin enough for the sun to filter through. Light showers may precipitate from them, but these clouds usually dissipate in the afternoon, leaving a clear night sky.

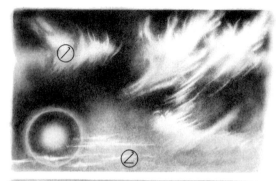

Stratus clouds:
The lowest of clouds, forming a uniform layer like fog in the air, they are often described as hill fog. Although not a normal rain cloud, they can produce drizzle. When they form thickly overnight and cover the morning sky they will usually be followed by a fine day.

Weather prediction

To be caught in bad weather can prove fatal. Learn to recognise signs that will enable you to make short-term weather predictions. This will help you decide whether to move on or to shelter.

▶ **Wildlife indicators:** Animals are sensitive to atmospheric pressure. Insect-eating birds, such as swallows, feed higher in good weather, lower when a storm is approaching. Unusual rabbit activity during the day, or squirrels taking more food than usual to the nest, may be a prelude to bad weather.

▶ **Fireside clues:** If camp fire smoke rises steadily, the weather is likely to remain fine. If it starts swirling, or being beaten downwards after rising a short way, a storm or shower is imminent.

▶ **Humans:** Curly-headed people find their hair becomes tighter and less manageable as bad weather approaches. Those with rheumatism, corns or similar ailments can usually tell when wet weather is coming by an increase in discomfort.

▶ **Sound and smell:** Sounds tend to carry further when wet weather is on the way, and the smell of vegetation becomes more distinctive before the arrival of rain.

▶ **Signs in the sky:** A red sky at night means rain is unlikely within the next two hours. A red sky in the morning indicates a storm is approaching. A grey morning heralds a dry day, and a grey evening sky means that rain is imminent. Early morning mist lifting from a valley is a sign of fair weather. In hilly country, if mist has not lifted by noon, it is set in for the day and will probably turn to rain during late afternoon. A clear night sky indicates good, settled weather, and possibly a frost at the end of summer.

Travel and terrain

Deciding which way to go will be influenced by your planned route, the information you have gathered on the ground, the fitness and endurance of your party, and by the nature of the terrain. Set a pace to suit the least able.

Maintaining direction

Having decided upon a direction, you must endeavour to maintain it. One way is to head towards a distant landmark. Orientation is more difficult in forests and dense vegetaton so skirt around them if possible and use a compass to get back on course. Rivers offer a clearly defined route. Where they cut through gorges it may be impossible to follow their banks, so take to high ground and cut off the bends. Where a river meanders widely on a plain, cut across the loop to avoid marshy areas. Once on high ground, stick to it until certain you have found the spur down that allows the best progress in your desired direction.

In featureless territory, if the group is three or more, maintain a straight line by spreading out a little and following in each other's tracks. Look back frequently: those behind you should be directly behind each other in a straight line. Move in relay — the one who goes ahead can rest while everyone else moves up from the rear.

If travelling alone, align yourself by looking back at your own tracks, if they are visible, or set up markers (sticks, piles of stones) at intervals in alignment with each other so that you can check that you are not deviating from your route.

Moving in groups

Always move in formation. It makes it easier to check that no stragglers have been left behind. Have a briefing before setting off to discuss the route and to designate rallying points at which to regroup.

Divide responsibilities

Appoint a scout to select the best route and find the easiest way to avoid obstacles. A number two should make sure the scout maintains correct overall direction. Both will need to be relieved frequently as it is tiring work.

The others should travel in pairs to ensure no one gets left behind. A head count and check on everyone's condition is vital after a river crossing or negotiating difficult terrain — check equipment too. Be especially careful to keep the group together in bad weather and if you have to travel at night.

Pace and progress

In estimating distance on foot, allow 3km (under 2 miles) per hour. If going uphill, reduce this by a third. Rest frequently and adjust loads which are uncomfortable. Repack if necessary. On average take a break of 10 minutes every 30–45 minutes, depending on the terrain and condition of the group.

The scout should not go too fast for those behind. After an obstacle they should wait and allow everyone to catch up.

Try to maintain a smooth, even pace — it is less tiring. Keep hands free to help maintain balance and break a fall. On steep ground, the pace should be shortened, on easy ground lengthened. Avoid overstepping on descents as it jars the body and

must know

Night vision
It takes 30-40 minutes for eyes to become accustomed to the dark. Once this is achieved, they must be protected from bright light or the night vision will be impaired. If a light must be used, cover one eye so that vision in that eye is retained. A red filter over a torch will help.

increases fatigue. On steep descents or slippery ground, use ropes to provide handholds.

Walking at night

Negotiating territory at night can be dangerous, but may be necessary in an emergency, or, for instance, in a desert where it is more comfortable to travel at night. Because it is difficult to see during night hours you are easily disoriented. It is always darker among trees so keep to open country if possible. When you come across an object at night, avoid looking directly at it: the edges will show more clearly than the dark mass at the centre, and in poor light objects at the edges of your vision are often seen more distinctly. Ears are good sensors in the dark — the sound of a river provides a guide to how fast it is flowing. Smells can also aid identification.

Walk slowly in the dark and test each step before putting all your weight forward. Use a shuffling step to go downhill.

Upland travel

In mountainous and hilly country, keep to high ground — it makes navigation easier. Rivers may be in steep-sided gullies and have rapids, falls and slippery rocks that are difficult to negotiate. Use spurs to

Do not follow a river as it winds in deep valleys through hilly country. By climbing from the valley at (a) and following the ridge, steep and tiring descents and climbs are avoided. At (b) a night halt is taken dropping down to the first available water source. This could provide shelter too, which may be unavailable on an exposed ridge. When a river gets larger and the valley opens out, drop down to follow the river banks once more (c).

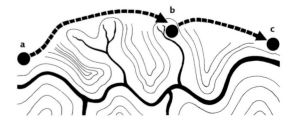

climb out of valleys and get on to ridges. You may have to drop down into valleys for shelter and to find water but do not go right to the valley bottom if you can find what you need on the way. Pockets of cold air get trapped in valley bottoms and you may be warmer and less tired if you choose a sheltered spot higher up. Be aware of fading light and your own flagging energy. Look for shelter before you are exhausted.

Steep slopes

Traverse slopes in a zig-zag. As you change direction always set off with the uphill foot to avoid crossing your legs over each other and losing balance. When climbing steep slopes lock your knees together after each step to rest the muscles.

To descend, keep your knees bent. Try to go straight down — lean back and dig in your heels if you are picking up too much speed. Avoid loose rock and scree. When climbing, test every foothold before

Abseiling

Loop rope around a firm anchor (test it with your full body weight). Avoid sharp edges. Pass both ends of the rope between your legs from the front, bring it round to the left of your body, over your right shoulder and down across your back. Hold the rope in front with your left hand and at the back with the right. Plant feet firmly against the slope about 45cm (18in) apart, and lean back. Let the rope around your body carry the weight. Do not try to support yourself with your upper hand. Step slowly downwards. Your lower hand controls rate of descent. Pay the rope out one hand at a time. Make sure you are in a firm position before hauling the rope down and that you have planned your next move. Once the rope is down you may have no way of retracing your steps. Abseiling can be dangerous. If possible, pad out shoulders and groin, and use gloves. Never attempt unless you are accompanied by an expert or in a survival situation.

putting your weight on it. Avoid stepping on stones
or logs that may dislodge.

With practice it is possible to jump down loose
ground provided there are no sudden drops. Keep
your feet square and a shoulder-width apart, dig in
your heels and slide. As you increase speed, jump and
start again before dirt builds up under your feet and
you lose control. For steep slopes, abseiling is safer.

Jungle travel

You may have to cut your way through dense jungle if
there is no way of going round. Chop downwards and
as low as possible at stems on both sides so that they
fall away from the path, not across it. Avoid leaving
spikes standing — bamboo points can be lethal.

Jungle vegetation is often covered in thorns and
spikes: go round the worst of it if you can. When snared,
back off and untangle. Rushing only makes it worse.

Waterways

A wide, navigable river is easier to float on than to
walk beside, provided you can make a suitable craft.

Rafts

To make a raft, use bamboo, uprooted trees that are
sound and unrotted, or the tops of the trunks of
deadfalls. Oil drums or other floating objects will
support the raft. Alternatively, a sheet of tarpaulin
can be secured to create a dry hollow between
floating drums in an improvised coracle.

When on the water, tie all equipment securely to
the raft or to a safety line. Everyone aboard should
have a bowline attached around the waist and
secured to a safety line or to the raft.

Bamboo raft

Cut thickish bamboo in 3m (10ft) lengths. Make holes through the canes near the ends and half-way along. Pass stakes through these holes to connect the canes. Lash each cane to the stakes with twine or vines. Make a second layer to fit on top of the first and lash the two together.

Gripper bar raft

Place two pliable strong stakes on the ground and lay logs over them. Place two more stakes on top. Tie each pair of stakes firmly together on one side. With a helper standing on top to force the other stake ends together, tie these so that the logs are gripped between them. Notching the ends of the gripper bars will stop the ropes from slipping.

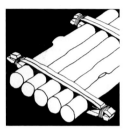

Steering

Make a paddle rudder and mount it on an A-frame near one end of the raft. Secure the A-frame with guy-lines to the corners of the raft and tie the rudder on to it so it does not slip. The rudder can also be used as a sweep for propulsion.

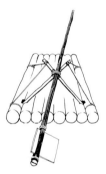

Bowline

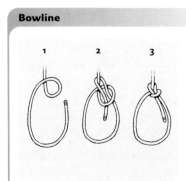

This knot makes a loop that will neither tighten nor slip under strain. Use it on the end of a lifeline or wherever such a fixed loop is needed.
1 Make a small loop a little way along from the end of the rope.
2 Bring the live end up through the loop, around the standing part and back down through the loop.
3 Pull on the live end to tighten, easing the knot into shape.

Travelling by raft

In a large group with several rafts, the first raft should carry no equipment or provisions, just the fittest group members to act as lookouts. Lifelines should be long enough to allow free movement, but not so long that they trail in the water. In swift-flowing rivers with dangerous rapids it is better not to tie on. If the raft gets out of control and is swept towards dangerous water, head for the bank. In shallow water the best means of controlling a raft is like a punt, but preferably with two long poles — one person poling at one front corner of the raft, and another at the diagonally opposite back corner.

Waterfalls and rapids are often indicated by a spray or mist and can be heard from some distance away. If in doubt, moor the raft and reconnoitre on foot. For a dangerous stretch of water, unload the raft and carry equipment downstream. Post someone to recover the raft where the river becomes safe again, then release it to drift down. It may need repairs, but at least you will be unhurt.

Never raft after dark. At night secure the raft firmly and make shelter on higher ground.

Crossing a river

If you have to cross a river, follow these simple rules:
▶ Look for places where the water is shallow enough to wade across. Test ahead with a pole for hidden depths.
▶ Find rocks to provide stepping stones, or leap from boulder to boulder across a stream bed.
▶ Head upstream for an easier crossing place if you find yourself at a river estuary, which will be wide with strong currents and subject to tides.

must know

Bogs, marshes and quicksand
If you cannot avoid crossing a marsh, jump from tuft to tuft of grass. Swim with a breast-stroke to firm ground if you find yourself sinking in a bog or quicksand. Do not try to jump. Spreading your body distributes your weight.

▶ If you do cross a wide stretch of river, especially near the sea, do not set off immediately opposite the point you hope to reach — make allowances for where the current will take you.

Study the water

Surface movement can indicate what lies beneath. The main flow of the current is evident from a chevron shape of smoother water round any projection (a), the V widening downstream.

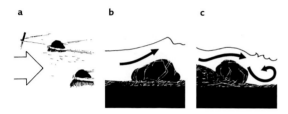

a   b   c

Waves that stay in one position on the surface (b) are evidence of a boulder on the bottom. An obstruction close to the surface creates an eddy downstream where surface water appears to run back against the main flow. If a large boulder coincides with a steep drop (c) these eddies can produce a powerful backward pull downstream of the obstruction. They can draw swimmers in and are very dangerous.

Tides and currents

Tides are caused by the counter-gravities of the sun and moon and vary according to both location and time of year. A line of debris along a beach indicates the high tide mark. Keep an eye on the rising water level to ensure you are not cut off. Look out for strong currents, especially off headlands. Where a beach falls steeply into deep water there will be a strong undertow. If you have to swim in this area, keep a safety line around your waist with someone anchoring you on shore. If a strong current forces you offshore, swim across the current, using side stroke to preserve energy. If facing large waves, let each one pass by submerging, and swim in the troughs towards shore.

Wading across

Never underestimate a stretch of water, however shallow. Cut a stick to aid balance and cross facing towards the current. Roll trousers up or take them off so they are dry for the other side. Keep boots on for grip. Undo the belt fastening of a back-pack so you can slip it off easily if you get swept over, but do not lose hold of it (it will almost certainly float and you can use it to right yourself).

Turn at a slight angle, your back towards the bank you want to reach — the current will move you in that direction. Shuffle sideways rather than taking strides. Use a stick to test for depth and try each foothold before transferring your weight.

A group wading across together should line up behind the strongest, each holding the one in front at the waist and moving in step. Alternatively, link arms side-by-side, holding on to a pole or branch to keep in alignment. Cross by facing the bank and moving forwards. Only the side of the first person opposes the current and the group provides stability for everyone.

Crossing with ropes

If a rope is available it can make wading safer — but you need a loop of rope three times as long as the width of the stream and there must be at least three people in the party. The fittest person crosses first while two control the rope to keep it out of the water as much as possible and to haul the crosser to safety if difficulties are encountered.

The person crossing is secured round the chest to the loop. The other two are not tied on — they pay out the rope as it is needed and can stop the crosser being washed away (a).

Flotation aids

▶ Use anything that floats: fuel cans, plastic bottles, logs.

▶ Put your clothes and belongings inside a waterproof bag, leaving an air space. Tie the neck, bend it over and tie again. Hold on to it, using your legs to propel yourself.

▶ Pile twigs and straw into the centre of a waterproof sheet to create air pockets, then pile clothes and equipment on top, tying securely. Do not attempt to sit on the bundles or place your weight on them.

▶ If four people lash their bags together they can be used to support an injured member of the party or a non-swimmer.

▶ If no waterproof material is available, make a small raft to float your things on. Bundle your belongings and, if heavy, make the raft two-layered so that only the lower layer sinks into the water and your kit stays dry.

When 1 reaches the bank, he unties himself and 2 ties on and crosses, controlled by the others. Any number of people can be sent across at this point (b).

When 2 has reached the bank, 3 ties on and crosses. 1 takes most of the strain; 2 stands by in case anything goes wrong (c).

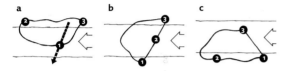

Swimming across

If you cannot swim do not try — rely on others to get you across with the help of some sort of float. Even the strongest swimmers should use a flotation aid to save energy and keep kit dry. Do not swim with your clothes on, you need something warm to put on at the other side.

Make sure your landing point has a beach or something to haul yourself out with. Avoid tangled branches where you might get trapped. Enter well upstream to allow for the current carrying you down river: better to overestimate and be a little longer in the water than to pass your landing place.

Check the strength of the current by watching floating logs and flotsam. Look for obstructions and eddies. If you hit weed in the water, adopt a crawl stroke to cut through it. Once a strong swimmer has cleared a passage, others can follow in that channel.

want to know more?

Take it to the next level...
- ▶ **For more on storms and weather changes** 134-9
- ▶ **For more on hot and cold climate health hazards** 187-8
- ▶ **For more on recovery after drowning** 166

Other sources...
- ▶ **Practise climbing techniques at a class or climbing wall before your trip.**
- ▶ **Take an orientation course or practise map reading on regular short outings.**
- ▶ **Check local weather offices for regional weather variations.**

must know

Currents and obstacles
When forced against an obstruction by the current you will feel its full force and may be unable to move. Look out for submerged obstacles and keep well away if you can.

5 Dangers

Dangerous situations are sometimes unavoidable. Knowing how to react can minimise their impact. This chapter provides a mini-guide to dealing with difficult situations you may come across, including severe storms, earthquakes, forest fires, avalanches and confrontations with dangerous animals.

Dangerous creatures

Few animals are likely to attack except in self-defence, but you may unintentionally provoke them. Avoid camping on an animal trail or close to a watering place. Keep a safe distance from dangerous sea and river creatures, snakes and insects.

Injured or cornered animals
A trapped animal can be dangerous. If you prevent them from escaping, you are forcing them to fight.

Bears

A bear can easily kill a person and a wounded bear is particularly dangerous. Bears frequently scavenge around homesteads in northern forests and are just as likely to come near your camp for easy pickings. Use noise to drive them off — do not get too close.

Crocodiles and alligators

Most float almost submerged with only eyes and nostrils breaking the surface of the water. They will attack large mammals including humans, pulling

Dangerous confrontations

Attacks by large animals are rare. Keep out of their way. If you confront one, it will be surprised and you may unintentionally provoke the animal to attack.

▶ If you come face to face with a large animal: freeze, slowly back off while talking in a calm manner, avoid sudden movements and keep calm. Remember that animals can smell fear.
▶ Move out of the way if the animal appears to charge. You may be blocking its escape route.
▶ If chased, zig-zag when you run — animals such as rhinos charge in a straight line and have poor eyesight.
▶ A skilled nocturnal predator such as a leopard or tiger sees moving objects well. If you freeze you are less likely to be seen.
▶ The final option is to climb a tree.

their prey beneath the surface to drown. On land, despite their short legs, they are capable of a considerable show of speed over short distances. They hunt mainly at night, sunning themselves during the day. Do not swim in crocodile or alligator areas, especially at night, and never during the rainy season — when most attacks occur.

Stags

Any of the large-horned animals is likely to be able to wound you with its horns before you can reach it with a weapon. Stags are particularly belligerent in the rutting season.

Wolves

A wolf may get curious and look at you from a distance. If you are badly injured and unable to defend yourself, wolves may finish you off, but stories of being chased by packs of ferocious wolves are exaggerated.

Apes and monkeys

The larger apes can easily kill a man but they are rarely aggressive animals and will usually give plenty of warning for you to back off. Small monkeys are more often encountered and more immediately dangerous — they have sharp teeth. Mature chimpanzees, in particular, can be bad-tempered.

Snakes and insects

Unless you accidentally come into contact with them, snakes will not be a threat. Regularly check clothing, bedding and equipment for reptiles or insects. Occasionally a snake or a centipede may be

good to know

Snake free
There are no poisonous snakes in New Zealand, Cuba, Haiti, Jamaica, Puerto Rico, Ireland, Polynesia and the polar regions.

Sustainable environments

Most of the animals you encounter in the wild could be a source of nourishment — they are a sustainable source of food. If you see wildlife, then you know the environment around you is sustainable.

attracted by your warmth. If you wake to find an unwelcome visitor inside your bed, try to remember that they are not attacking. Move gently and calmly to free yourself. Keep clothing and footwear off the ground, and always shake them before putting them on.

If you disturb a bee, wasp or hornet nest, any bare flesh, including your face, is vulnerable to attack. The best course of action is to run away. Perspiration will attract insects looking for salt. Protect your armpits and groin area. At dawn and dusk, wear a net over your head to protect yourself from mosquitos, or cover your head with a tee-shirt impregnated with repellent. In camp, burn green wood or leaves to make a smoky fire — it will help keep insects at bay.

---

must know

Snake safety rules
- **Stay calm if you encounter a snake:** Do not move suddenly or strike at it. Back off slowly. Do not approach, even if it seems to be dead. Some only move to strike when prey is close.
- **Watch where you step:** After eating, and when shedding their skin, snakes are sluggish and more easily trodden on. Look closely before parting bushes or picking fruit. Some snakes are arboreal.
- **Never tease, pick up or corner:** Some snakes, such as the Bushmaster of South and Central America, Black Mamba of Africa and King Cobra of Asia will attack when cornered or guarding a nest.
- **Protect bare hands:** Use a stick to turn over stones or for digging.
- **Wear stout boots:** The teeth of many snakes are too small to penetrate them.
- **Check bedding, clothes and packs before putting them on:** Snakes may use them as shelter.
- **Use a stick to kill:** If you have to kill a snake use a long stick to make a single chopping blow to the back of the head. Make it effective first time — a wounded snake is very dangerous.

Fish

Many reef fish have toxic flesh. The poisons are present in all parts of the fish, but especially in the liver, intestines and eggs. Other fish can be dangerous to touch: Ray fish have a poisonous barb in their tail; Stonefishes and Toadfishes have venomous spines; Electric Eels deliver an electric shock; Jellyfish trail long 'streamers' in the water that can carry dangerous and painful toxins.

There are also a number of aggressive fish. The bold and inquisitive Barracuda has been known to attack man. The Sea Bass, which can grow to 1·8m (5.5ft), and the Moray Eel, which has many sharp teeth and grows to 1·5m (5ft), can be aggressive if disturbed. Sea snakes are venomous. Though unlikely to bite, they should not be approached.

Sharks

Few types of shark are considered dangerous. Six sharks account for most human casualties: the Great White, Mako, Tiger, Hammerhead, Bull and Grey Nurse (see the colour section for illustrations).

Sharks in tropical oceans have abundant food and are rarely ferocious. They can usually be scared off by a jab of a stick, especially on the nose. Sharks mostly feed off the ocean bottom, but hungry sharks will follow fish to the surface and into shallow water, where they can be dangerous. Sharks feed most actively at night and at dusk and dawn. Their small eyes have limited vision and they locate prey by smell and vibrations in the water. They are attracted by blood from wounds, body wastes and rubbish. Weak and fluttery movements will draw a shark's attention because they suggest a vulnerable, wounded creature.

Shark behaviour

If a shark keeps its distance, it is only curious. If it circles inwards and begins sudden movement, an attack is likely.

good to know

Evading a shark
Sharks have difficulty stopping suddenly or turning quickly. A good swimmer can evade a single large shark by making rapid changes of direction.

It will be repelled by strong, regular movements and loud noises. A group of clothed humans bunched together will be safer than a single individual.

Protection against sharks

▶ If you have shark repellent, follow the manufacturer's instructions. Use only if the situation is grave. Repellent soon dissipates in the water and becomes ineffective. Choose your moment well — you may not have a second chance.

▶ If sharks are present try to avoid passing body wastes. If you vomit try to hold it in the mouth and reswallow, or throw it as far away as possible.

▶ If it is necessary to swim, use strong regular strokes and avoid schools of fish.

▶ If a group of people is threatened they should bunch together and face outwards. To ward off attack kick outwards and punch out with a stiff arm using the heel of the hand. Make loud noises by slapping the water with cupped hands and shouting under the surface.

▶ If you have a knife, be prepared to use it — go for the snout, gills or eyes.

▶ On a raft or boat, do not fish when sharks are around and do not throw waste overboard. Do not trail arms or legs in the water. If a shark threatens to attack, discourage it with jabs to the snout with a paddle or pole.

False alarm

Not every fin showing above the surface is attached to a shark. The wing tips of large rays may resemble a pair of sharks moving in synchronisation. The fins or flippers of whales, porpoises and dolphins may also break the surface.

Spiders and other dangerous creatures

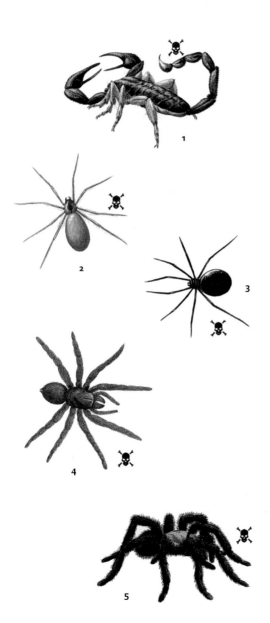

1 Scorpion:
Found in tropical, subtropical and warm temperate areas. Mainly nocturnal. The sting is in the tail. Some kinds can inflict a fatal bite, but this is rare.

2 Recluse or Fiddleback Spider:
Found in North America. Bite is rarely fatal, but tissue degeneration around wound can cause disfigurement or amputation if untreated.

3 Black Widow or Hourglass Spider:
Found in warm areas over much of the world. Recognisable by red, yellow or white markings on abdomen. Bite may disable victim for up to a week, but rarely fatal.

4 Funnelweb:
Found in Australia. Nocturnal. A bite can kill.

5 Tarantula:
Found in tropical America (one kind in southern Europe). Bite is painful but the poison is fairly mild and not disabling.

Spiders and other dangerous creatures

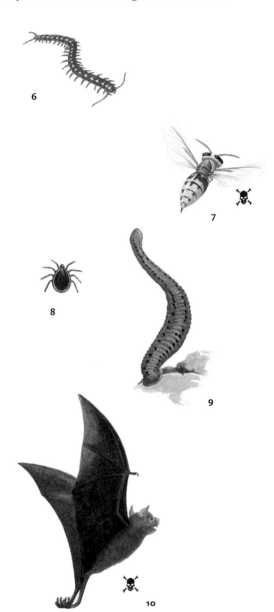

6 Centipede and millipede:
Some tropical and desert kinds have a poisonous bite. Brush off in the direction they are moving — there is less chance of sharp claws digging into you.

7 Hornet:
Some tropical kinds are very aggressive and poisonous. Several stings at once could prove fatal.

8 Tick:
Common in the tropics. The small biting head eats into a wound. Do not pull off: use heat, petrol, alcohol or hot water to make it drop off.

9 Leech:
Found in tropical jungles and other moist areas. These are blood-suckers and they carry infection. Do not pull off: remove with fire or a pinch of salt.

10 Vampire Bat:
Found in Central and South America. Nocturnal, they suck blood from sleeping victims. Bites may carry rabies.

Poisonous snakes and lizards

The Americas

1 Rattlesnake:
Found in all parts of North America. The rattle on the end of the tail is usually, but not always, sounded as a warning. The largest kinds are the Diamondbacks (over 2.1m, 7ft), with distinctive diamond-shaped blotches.

2 Copperhead:
Found in eastern United States. Fairly timid. Bites are rarely fatal.

3 Cottonmouth or Water Moccasin:
Found in and by freshwater, southern United States. Belligerent — do not annoy!

4 Tropical Rattlesnake:
Found in South America, north to Mexico. Nocturnal. Large, aggressive, very dangerous.

5 Fer de Lance:
Found in South America, north to Mexico. Causes many deaths. Some are arboreal. All loop their body before striking.

6 Bushmaster:
Found in Central and South America. Averages 2–2.6m (6–8ft). Nocturnal. Vicious if cornered; the most feared of all New World snakes.

7 Coral Snake:
From southern United States into South America. Small-mouthed, reluctant to bite but deadly.

8 Gila Monster:
Found in deserts of Arizona, Mexico and nearby. Has a poisonous bite.

9 Beaded Lizard:
Found in arid parts of Mexico and Central America. Do not handle: poisonous bite.

5 Dangers

Poisonous snakes and lizards

Europe

10 Adder:
Found especially on heaths, moors and open areas, into mountains. Relatively small (30-75cm, 12-30in). The only poisonous snake of northern Europe. Bites are hardly ever fatal. Has larger and more dangerous relatives in southern Europe.

Africa and Asia

11 Puff Adder:
Found in semi-arid areas, often near water, in Africa and Arabian Peninsula.

12 Saw-scaled Viper:
Found in arid areas of North Africa, west to India. Causes many fatalities.

13 Russell's Viper:
Found in Pakistan, east to Taiwan. Common and the cause of most viper bites in the area.

14 Malay Pit Viper or Moccasin: Found in southeast Asia and Indonesia. A frequent cause of bites. Many types: avoid any that resemble it.

15 Cobra: Occurs in Africa, east to India. Average 1.5-2m (5-6ft). When alarmed is recognisable by the raised head and spreading hood.

16 Boomslang:
In trees and very hard to spot, in Africa, south of the Sahara. Highly venomous. Inflates its throat when alarmed.

17 Krait:
Found from India to Indonesia. Nocturnal. Bites are often fatal.

18 Mamba:
Found in Africa, south of the Sahara. Average 1.5-2.1m (5-7ft). Usually in trees but the large Black Mamba is mainly terrestrial. Often quick to strike. Fatal in almost all untreated cases.

Poisonous snakes and lizards

Australasia

19 Death Adder:
Found in sandy areas, Australia, Papua New Guinea and nearby islands. Small (45–60cm, 18–24in). Well camouflaged; highly venomous, but not as dangerous as the Tiger Snake and Taipan.

20 Australian Black Snake:
Found in or near fresh water over most parts of Australia. Very rarely fatal. Flattens its neck when aroused.

21 Australian Brown Snake:
Found in drier parts, Australia and Papua New Guinea. Aggressive and very poisonous.

22 Tiger Snake:
Found in semi-arid areas, Australia and Tasmania. Aggressive, very poisonous, the principal cause of fatal bites.

23 Sea Snake:
Occurs in Indian and Pacific oceans; some in estuaries and coastal swamps. Scales distinguish them from eels. Not aggressive, but some kinds are the most venomous snakes of all.

24 Taipan:
Found in northern Australia. Large: may grow to 3.5m (11ft). Ferocious when provoked. Deadly poisonous.

Dangerous water creatures

River dangers

1 Electric Eel:
Native to Orinoco and Amazon river systems of South America. Prefers shallow water. The shock from a large one — 2m (7ft) long — can be 500 volts: enough to knock someone down.

2 Piranha:
Found in Orinoco, Amazon and Parguay river systems of South America. May grow up to 50cm (20in) long. Razor-sharp interlocking teeth can be very dangerous.

Sea and river dangers

3 Stingray:
Found in shallow tropical waters, a few kinds in rivers in tropical South America and West Africa. Distinctive ray shape. Venomous spines in tail can inflict severe, sometimes fatal, injury.

Saltwater dangers

4 Rabbitfish or Spinefeet:
Found mainly on reefs in Indian and Pacific Oceans. Edible but with sharp venomous spines in most fins.

5 Tang or Surgeonfish:
Found in all tropical waters. Lancet-like spines on sides of tail can inflict severe wounds.

Dangerous water creatures

6

7

8

9

10

11

6 Venomous Toadfish:
Found in tropical waters off coasts of Central and South America. Lies buried in sand and has sharp, very poisonous spines on the back.

7 Scorpionfish or Zebrafish:
Found mostly on reefs in tropical Indian and Pacific Oceans. A sting is intensely painful. Less potent relatives in Mediterranean and Atlantic.

8 Stonefish:
Found in tropical Pacific and Indian Oceans. Drab appearance makes it almost impossible to see. When trodden on, dorsal spines inject venom that is agonizingly painful, in the worst cases fatal.

9 Weeverfish:
Lies buried in sand off coasts of Europe south to West Africa and the Mediterranean. Venomous spines on back and gills produce disabling pain. Soothe it by applying very hot water.

Poisonous to eat

10 Porcupine Fish:
Found in all shallow tropical waters. Different types. When alarmed, inflates into a very spiny ball. Flesh is poisonous.

11 Puffer Fish:
Found in all tropical and many warmer temperate waters. When alarmed it puffs up into a ball. Blood, liver and gonads are poisonous: 28mg (1oz) can kill.

Dangerous water creatures

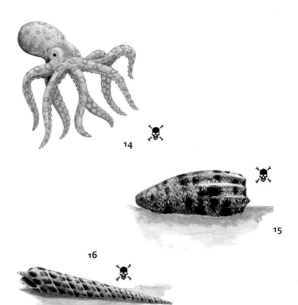

12 Triggerfish:
Found in shallow tropical seas.
Many kinds are poisonous to eat.
Other sea creatures
13 Portuguese Man-of-war:
Not a jellyfish but a colony of
hydroids. Mainly sub-tropical but
common in Gulf Stream, which
may take it to British shores.
Tentacles, which carry stinging
cells, can stream out for 12m
(40ft). Not fatal but enough to
incapacitate a person.
14 Blue-ringed Octopus:
Small, sometimes only fist-sized,
found off eastern Australia.
Potentially lethal bite if trodden
on. Treat all tropical reef
octopuses with caution.
15 Cone Shell:
Subtropical and tropical
gastropods, with venomous
harpoon-like barb. Do not touch.
16 Auger or Terebra Shell:
Found in temperate and tropical
seas, particularly the Indo-Pacific.
Has a stinging barb.

Sharks and dangerous fish

1 Great White Shark: Grows to 6m (18ft), grey back, white belly, with black eyes and stubby conical snout. Common off southern Africa, east and west North America and southern Australia and New Zealand.
2 Mako: Averages 2–3m (6–9ft), ultramarine blue back, creamy-white belly. Common in temperate seas of Australia, New Zealand and South Africa. A fast swimmer; occasionally leaps out of water. **3 Tiger Shark:** Averages 3–3.5m (12–13.5ft), greyish-brown back, white belly, with a wide head and jaws and abruptly squared-off snout. Common in tropical and subtropical oceans, often close inshore. **4 Barracuda:** Thin, torpedo-like fish (not a shark). Bluish-barred back, silver belly, with a protruding mouth packed with sharp teeth. Some kinds grow to 2m (7ft). Found in tropical waters. Very fast, often in shoals. Usually dangerous only when there is blood in the water. **5 Hammerhead:** Found in tropical and subtropical waters. Distinctively flattened hammer-like head. Several kinds, the largest reaching 6m (18ft). **6 Bull Shark:** Found in tropical west Atlantic with close relatives off southern Africa and in Indian Ocean. Grey above and white below, up to 4m (12ft). Aggressive, and dangerous in its liking for shallow water and ability to ascend far up rivers. **7 Nurse:** The Grey Nurse of eastern Australian waters reaches over 4m (13ft). Greyish back and white belly. Often found very close inshore.

Avalanches

Avalanches are a serious hazard in all high mountain regions. They most frequently occur on steep slopes of between 20° and 60°, especially between 30° and 45°, and usually within 24 hours of a snow fall.

Causes of avalanches

Avalanches can be triggered by temperature change, noise and various coincidental conditions. If you are travelling to an avalanche-prone area you should be aware of these causes.

Avoid steep ground where fresh snow has just fallen. After a major fall, wait 24 hours for it to settle. Rain, or a rise in temperature, after a snow fall greatly increases the risk of avalanche — the melting process lubricates the slide. Heavy snow during low temperatures may not have time to stabilise and can cause an avalanche. Avoid slopes with rocks — the rocks could fall and set off an avalanche. On a convex slope the gravitational movement downward compacts the snow at the bottom and creates tension at the top, making it more likely to slip. Where snow is building up on the lee side of a ridge, or the head of a steep gully, it is also under tension and the slightest disturbance can cause it to slide.

Finding a safe route

Slopes with irregular surfaces and timbered slopes are safest. Slopes with rocky outcrops and trees are safer to cross than bare ones. Carefully choose the best place to cross and test the snow with a stick or ice axe. On dangerous ground, rope together and secure the rope to a fixed object, such as a large rock or pin fixing. Let one person go across the dangerous areas alone, paying out the rope as he goes, and securing himself at the other end before the next person crosses.

Avalanche precautions

Take the following precautions to minimise the risk of being caught in an avalanche:

▶ The heat of the sun on the snow can cause avalanches. Before noon, travel in shaded areas and keep off slopes exposed to the sun. After noon, keep to slopes that have already been exposed, avoiding those now in the sun for the first time.

▶ Avoid small gullies and valleys with steep side walls, especially after a snow fall.

▶ Stick to ridges and high ground above avalanche paths — you are more likely to trigger a slide but have a better chance of being on top of the debris or not being carried down by the slide.

▶ Find out about past avalanche activity as a guide to where other avalanches are likely.

Convex slope   **Concave slope**

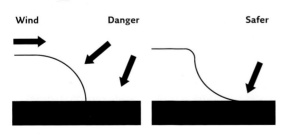

Wind   Danger   Safer

Never make camp on the lee side of a convex slope. A concave slope is safer.

Starting avalanches

The majority of victims of avalanches start them off themselves. Stay alert.

Mud slide

A mud slide is similar to an avalanche, but instead of tons of snow, masses of mud sliding on water buries all in its path. Avoid low-lying areas and water courses. Stay on the spurs and ridges. If caught up in a slide, use swimming actions to stay on top and go feet first.

Forest fires

Carelessness with lighted cigarettes and burning matches is the cause of many forest fires. Sun shining through an abandoned bottle or a piece of broken glass can also start a blaze in a dry season. The best protection from fire is prevention.

Escape route

The first sign of an approaching forest fire will be the smell of smoke. Then you will probably hear the fire before you see flames. You may notice unusual animal behaviour.

Unless the fire is so close that you have no choice, do not immediately flee. Choose your escape route. Check the surrounding terrain and the wind direction to assess the possible spread of the fire. Smoke will indicate the direction of the wind — the fire will travel fastest in that direction. If the wind is blowing away from you, towards the fire, move into the wind. Fire travels faster uphill so do not make for high ground. Try to go around the fire but if you cannot skirt or outdistance it then take refuge in a large clearing, deep ravine, watercourse or gulley. A river is the best fire break — even if the flames can leap across you will be reasonably safe in the water. Do not discard clothes — they will shield you from the full force of radiated heat.

Into the fire

Sometimes the best escape route may be to run through the flames. This will be impossible if the flames are intense and the fire covers a large area. But if the fire is less dense, it may be possible to run through it to refuge on the burned-out land on the other side. Cover as much exposed skin as you can and use water to wet clothing, hair and any uncovered flesh. Dampen a piece of cloth to cover your nose and mouth.

Going to earth
If there is no natural break or gully in which to shelter and the fire is too deep to think of running through it, as a last resort you may have to seek the protection of the earth. People have survived fierce fires by digging themselves in and covering themselves with earth, allowing the fire to burn over the top of them. The risk is great, not just from heat but from suffocation: fire burns up oxygen.

Scrape as much of a hollow as you can, throwing the earth on to a coat or cloth if you have one, then pull the cloth over you with its earth covering. Cup your hands over your mouth and nose and breathe through them. This will cool down and filter the very hot air and sparks, which can damage the respiratory system. Try to hold your breath as the fire passes over.

Fighting a forest fire
Forestry plantations usually have racks of fire-beating equipment at intervals along the main routes. This consists of brooms and spade-shaped beaters. Use them to put out the beginnings of a blaze. Do not beat rapidly — it will only fan the flames and spread sparks. The object is to smother the fire by bringing the beater down over the flames to extinguish them. If no equipment is available, use a coat or blanket or a leafy branch to beat it out.

Stay in a vehicle

If caught in a forest fire in a vehicle, stay inside and keep the windows shut. Turn off the ventilation system. The car will give you some protection from radiant heat. Drive away from the fire if you can but, if immobilised, stay put.
People have survived by staying in a vehicle until the glass began to melt, by which time the fire had moved beyond them. If they had panicked and run into the fire they would have died.
There is a danger of the petrol tank exploding but your chances of surviving are greater than outside if the fire is intense and surrounding the vehicle.

Storms and floods

Out in the open you are particularly exposed to the ferocity of storms. Learn to recognise the signs of approaching bad weather. Be prepared to protect yourself at short notice.

Flash floods
Keep out of valley bottoms and stream beds both during and after heavy rainfall. Remember that you do not have to be at the bottom of a hill to be caught by water rushing down it — often carrying mud and a deadly debris of broken trees and rocks.

Lightning

The release of electrical charges built up in clouds can be especially dangerous on high ground or when you are the tallest object. In a lightning storm keep away from hill brows, tall trees and lone boulders. Make for low, level ground and lie flat.

Insulation

If you cannot get away from tall objects, but have dry material which will provide insulation, sit on it. Rubber-soled shoes may help insulation but are not a guarantee that you will be safe. A dry coil of climbing rope makes good insulation. Do not sit on anything wet. Bend your head down and hug your knees to your chest, lifting your feet off the ground and drawing in all extremities.

Stay low

You can sometimes sense that a lightning strike is imminent by a tingling in the skin and the sensation of hair standing on end. If you are standing up, drop to the ground at once, to lie flat, going first to your knees with your hands touching the ground. If you should be struck, the charge may take the easiest route to the earth through your arms — missing the torso and possibly saving you from heart failure or asphyxiation. Do not hold metal objects when there is lightning about and keep away from metal structures and fences. Proximity to large metal objects can be dangerous, even without contact: the shockwave generated by the heated air — as the lightning passes — can cause damage to the lungs.

must know

Drinking water
During a flood, drinking water supplies may become contaminated. Collect rainwater and boil any other water before you drink it.

Seek shelter

One of the best places to shelter in a lightning storm is at least 3m (10ft) inside a deep cave with a minimum space of 1m (4ft) on either side of you. Do not shelter in a cave mouth or under an overhang of rock in mountainous country. The lightning can spark across the gap.

Flood

Flooding may be caused by the overflowing of rivers, lakes and reservoirs due to heavy rains; by the build-up of sea or lake water due to the effects of submarine earthquake, hurricanes and freak high-tides and winds; or by the collapse of dams or dykes.

Heavy rain can rapidly produce torrents where there was a dry riverbed. Persistent rainfall over a long period after a dry spell should alert you to keep clear of water channels and low-lying ground, but a flood can affect much wider areas. It is always safer to camp on a spur. If the water is rising, move to higher ground. In hilly areas avoid valley bottoms — they are particularly prone to flash floods.

Flooded buildings

If you are in a solid building when the water begins to rise, stay where you are if it is rising rapidly. You will be less at risk than trying to evacuate on foot. Turn off gas and electricity and prepare emergency food supplies, warm clothing, candles and matches. Collect drinking water, in well-sealed containers to avoid spillage or contamination, and if possible a torch, whistle, mirror and brightly coloured cloths or flags to use for signalling. A camp stove is valuable for heating food and drinks, and for warmth.

Move to an upper floor, or on to the roof if necessary. If forced to occupy the roof, erect a shelter. If the roof is sloping, tie everyone to a chimneystack or other solid structure. If the water continues to rise, prepare a raft. Use bed sheets if you have no ropes to tie things together. Unless the water threatens to wash the building away, or rises so high that you are forced to evacuate, stay until it stops rising.

On the move
When walking or driving in flooded country:
▶ Remember that a small drop in the level of a flooded roadway can make a considerable difference to water depth.
▶ Do not attempt to cross water unless you are certain that it will not be higher than the centre of the car's wheels or higher than your knees if walking.
▶ If you must cross: use river-crossing techniques (see pages 110-13).
▶ Take special care when crossing submerged bridges. Part of the bridge may have been swept away by the flood waters.

Coastal flooding
A combination of high tides and winds can cause coastal flooding. Flood warnings will usually be given and evacuation is the best action.

Hurricanes

A hurricane is a wind of high speed — above force 12 on the Beaufort Scale — which brings torrential rain and can destroy any flimsy structures. It is a tropical form of cyclone, which in more temperate latitudes would be prevented from developing in the upper levels of the air by prevailing westerly winds.

Hurricanes develop over the ocean when sea temperatures are at their highest, especially in late summer. Warm air creates a low pressure core around which winds may rotate at speeds of 300kph (200mph) or more, circling anti-clockwise in the northern hemisphere, clockwise in the southern. The strongest winds are usually 16-19km (10-12 miles) from the centre of the hurricane but the centre, or 'eye', brings temporary calm. The eye may be from 6-50km (4-30 miles) across. The largest hurricanes are up to 500km (300 miles) in diameter. They can travel as fast as 50kph (30mph) wreaking devastation on islands and along shorelines they pass over, but usually slowing down when they reach the mainland to a speed of about 16kph (10mph).

Hurricane warnings

Meteorologists use satellites to track the progress of hurricanes and give warning of their approach. Some hurricanes move very erratically, so sailors particularly should monitor forecasts in hurricane areas.

Without a radio to alert you, a growing swell can be an indication of a hurricane — when coupled with other conditions such as highly coloured sunsets or sunrises, dense cirrus cloud converging towards the storm vortex, and abnormal rises and rapid drops in barometric pressure.

Hurricanes

Hurricanes are known by various names around the world:
Hurricane: Caribbean and North Atlantic, eastern North Pacific, western South Pacific.
Cyclone: Arabian Sea, Bay of Bengal, southern Indian Ocean.
Typhoon: China Sea, western North Pacific.
Willy-willy: Northwest Australia.

Safety precautions — hurricanes

Take the following precautions:

▶ Warnings are usually issued within 24 hours of an
expected hurricane. Get out of the hurricane's path
if you can.

▶ Keep away from river banks and the coast, where
destruction from flooding and tidal waves will be worst.

▶ Secure any objects that might be blown away.

▶ At sea take down all canvas, batten down hatches
and stow gear.

▶ If you are in a solid building and on high ground,
stay where you are: travel in a hurricane is extremely
dangerous. The safest place is usually the cellar or
under the stairs. Store drinking water — water and
power supplies may be cut off by the storm — and
have a battery-operated radio to receive any
instructions issued. If not in a sturdy structure,
evacuate to a hurricane shelter. Shut off power
supplies before you leave.

▶ Outdoors a cave will offer the best protection. A
ditch will be next best. If unable to escape, lie flat on
the ground to avoid flying debris. Shelter on the lee
side of a solid windbreak such as a stable rocky
outcrop or a wide belt of large trees. Beware of small
trees and fences, which could be uprooted.

Tornadoes

Tornadoes are the most violent of atmospheric
phenomena and the most destructive over a small
area. They develop when air at the surface has been
warmed and a column of air descends from the base
of cumulonimbus storm clouds above. Air rushing
into the low pressure area begins to rotate fiercely.
Wind speeds have been estimated at 620kph (400mph).

The diameter of the 'twister' at ground level is usually only 25–50m (80–160ft) but, within it, the destruction is enormous. Everything in its path, except the most solid structures, is sucked up into the air. The difference in pressure outside and inside a building is often the cause of its collapse — or 'explosion'.

Tornadoes travel at 50–65kph (30–40mph) and sound like a spinning top or engine — they have been heard up to 40km (25 miles) away. Sometimes they develop in a hurricane. At sea tornadoes produce waterspouts.

must know

Get out of the way
You can see and hear a tornado coming. Move at right angles to its apparent path.

Safety precautions — tornadoes
Take the following precautions:
▶ Find shelter in the most solid structure available — reinforced concrete or steel-framed, preferably in a storm cellar or cave. In a cellar, stay close to an outside wall, or in a specially reinforced section. If there is no basement, go to the centre of the lowest floor, or into a small room or shelter under sturdy furniture — but not where there is heavy furniture on the floor above. Keep away from windows.
▶ Close all doors and windows on the side facing the oncoming whirlwind and open those on the opposite side. This will prevent the roof lifting off and the house 'exploding'.
▶ Do not stay in a caravan or car: they could be drawn up by the storm.
▶ Outdoors you are vulnerable to flying debris and to being lifted up (though people have been lowered to the ground again unharmed). Take shelter in a ditch or depression in the ground, lie flat and cover your head with your arms.

Earthquakes

Earthquakes come suddenly with little warning. They range from minor vibrations in the earth, detectable only on delicate measuring instruments, to catastrophic upheavals. Animals become very alert, tense and ready to run.

Earthquake belts

Minor earth tremors can happen anywhere, but major quakes are confined to known earthquake belts where buildings should be planned to withstand them or to cause little damage if they do collapse. Sadly, buildings in these areas are rarely strong enough to withstand a quake. Major earthquakes can be predicted by seismologists, and some evacuation may be possible.

Safety precautions

If you have warning of a possible earthquake:
▶ Stay tuned to a local radio station for reports and advice.
▶ If inside a building, turn off gas, electricity and water when advised to do so. Stay indoors unless you have time to evacuate to an open area.
▶ Store breakable objects and take down large light fittings.
▶ Have ready: fresh water and emergency food, a torch, first aid materials and a fire extinguisher.
▶ In the open, keep away from anything that might fall on you: trees, buildings, etc.

Tsunami

A tsunami is a long high sea wave or series of waves resulting from an earthquake beneath the ocean.

The waves can reach more than 30m (100ft) high and cause considerable damage along coasts. A feature mainly of the Pacific, their effect and scale vary according to direction, shape of shoreline and other factors. A relatively small tsunami on one beach can be a giant wave a few miles along the coast.

Safety precautions

Not all earthquakes cause tsunami, but any earthquake could. Keep away from shores and take to higher ground when there are tremors. Do not go to look for a tsunami — if you are close enough to see the wave, you are probably too close to escape it.

What to do if an earthquake strikes

Indoors:
- Stay indoors. Douse fires. Stay away from windows and other glass.
- A lower floor or a cellar probably gives the best chance of survival. Make sure there are plenty of exits.
- Shelter beneath a table or other strong piece of furniture.

In a car:
- Stop as quickly and safely as you can.
- Stay in the car. It will offer some protection from falling objects. Crouch down below seat level.
- When the tremors cease, keep a watch for any obstructions and hazards: broken cables, undermined roadways or bridges.

Outdoors:
- Lie flat on the ground. Do not try to run (you will be thrown about and could be swallowed in a fissure).
- Keep away from tall buildings or any structures that might collapse.
- Do not go into a tunnel where you could be trapped.
- On a hillside it is safer to get to the top. Slopes are liable to landslide.
- In case of tidal waves, which often follow a quake, move off beaches to higher ground.

---

want to know more?

Take it to the next level...
- **For more on treating animal bites** 185-6
- **For more on treating burns** 176-7
- **For more on crossing water** 110-13
- **For more on tides and currents** 111

Other sources...
- **Invest in a guide to dangerous creatures. Study their habits and habitats; visit wildlife centres to see them in the flesh.**
- **Take a forestry course in fire-fighting.**
- **For severe weather warnings or avalanche activity, contact the local meteorological office. Some services provide warning calls to your mobile phone.**

6 Rescue

When rescue is needed, your first priority will be to let others know your situation and location. This chapter explains how to put out a distress signal and a coded message, the procedures followed by search parties so you can anticipate their whereabouts, and the preparations you should make for an air or sea rescue.

Signalling

Signalling is used to attract attention when you need help. The obvious method is to use a mobile phone or transmitter. If you have no such equipment, signals should be placed where they will be seen by rescue parties. Always use signals that will be easily understood.

must know

Distress signals
Almost any signal repeated six times will serve as a distress signal. Wait for one minute between each group of six signals. Repeat until you receive a response.

Distress signals

SOS (Save Our Souls) is an internationally recognised distress signal. It can be written, transmitted by radio, spelt out by semaphore or sent in Morse code. Mayday (from *m'aidez* — French for *help me*) is the signal used in radio-telecommunications. The International Mountain Distress Signal (apart from signalling SOS) is six whistles a minute (or six waves, light flashes, etc) followed by a minute's silence, then repeated.

Transmitters

Dinghies, liferafts and even personal lifejackets are sometimes equipped with transmitters, which send out bleeps indicating position. These and other emergency radio transmitters may be limited

Transmitter frequencies

Ship and plane transmitters can operate on many wavelengths, but some emergency equipment is set to fixed-frequency distress channels. Portable VHF transceivers used by mountaineering teams can communicate only with stations in a direct line of sight and without any intervening obstruction (though a relay station may be established on a high point). These sets are usually tuned to a mountain rescue frequency.

in range. To avoid wasting batteries, use only when there is a chance of signals being picked up. With long-range radio equipment, distress signals should be transmitted at regular intervals.

Fire signals

Fire — both flames and smoke — is an excellent way of attracting attention. Three fires is an internationally recognised distress signal. Place the fires in a triangle equal distances apart. If fuel is scarce, use only your campfire.

Signal fires should be prepared, kept dry, and ready to light when an aircraft passes nearby. Use tinder to get them going quickly. Petrol can be used as a firelighter but do not pour it on the fire. Lay a piece of petrol-soaked rag among the tinder, carry the fuel can a safe distance away and wait a few seconds before lighting the wick. If the fire does not light first time, pull the tinder apart, checking for sparks or embers, before adding more petrol.

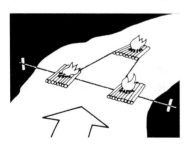

If by a lake or river, build rafts to place your fires on and anchor or tether them securely in position. (The direction of the current is shown by the arrow.)

Torch trees

Small isolated trees make good fire signals. Build a fire between the boughs using dry twigs and old birds' nests. The fire will ignite the foliage and produce plenty of smoke. If a tree is dead, start a fire at its base. It will burn for a long time.

Collecting fuel

In a large group, organise people to gather fuel. Signal fires should be built as soon as you have treated any injuries and made a shelter.

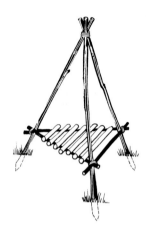

Keep the tripod well maintained and ready to light at a moment's notice. Drive the pole ends into the ground to prevent tipping over in strong winds. A burning cone fire can be seen for miles.

Luminous cone fires

On a clear and open site make a tripod with a platform to support a fire. The platform keeps the tinder and firewood off damp ground. Cover the structure with evergreen boughs: they will burn brightly and give off smoke. Place a brightly-coloured material on top of the cone fire — a parachute is ideal — which will be noticeable during the day. Whip it off when you ignite the fire.

Smoke indicators

By day smoke is a good locator. Have plenty of smoke-producing material ready to put on your fires: green boughs, oil, rubber, etc. Make sure the smoke is downwind of any potential landing site and of any other signals or codes you have arranged so they are not obscured from above.

▶ Light smoke is more visible against dark earth or dark green forest. Use green grass, leaves, moss and ferns. Wet materials smoulder for a long time, e.g. damp mats and seat covers. The smoke also keeps insects at bay.

▶ Dark smoke shows best against snow or desert sand. Use rubber or oil to produce it. If atmospheric conditions make the smoke hang in layers along the ground, build up the fire to increase its heat. Thermal currents will take the smoke to a good height where it will be more visible.

Vehicle or aircraft wreckage

If you are stranded with a broken vehicle or downed aircraft, the wreckage may provide many useful signalling aids. Supplies of fuel, oil and hydraulic fluid can be burned. Add tyres and electrical insulation to fires to generate black smoke. Glass and chrome make great reflectors. Lifejackets, dinghies and parachutes are brightly coloured and eye-catching — arrange them around your location where they will be most visible and attract attention.

Use wreckage to help fire signalling

Stand a fire on a piece of metal. It will keep kindling off damp ground, and when the metal gets hot it increases convection and makes the fire burn brightly. If polished, the metal will act as a reflector, intensifying the brightness.

Lights

Switch lights on at night. If batteries are running low, keep lights in reserve and use when you hear a passing aircraft or approaching rescue party. A series of six light flashes serves as a distress signal.

Noise

Noise is an excellent way of attracting attention if you know that people are within earshot. Use a whistle or improvise something that makes a noise that carries. A shout may be enough to get you noticed if you are trapped, or near help but too injured to reach it.

Be imaginative

On a river a noticeable floating object carrying a message may attract attention, for instance a small raft with a bright sail labelled 'SOS'. Attach a message to the raft inside a waterproof container, giving your location and situation. This is just one example of the many ways to attract help.

must know

Where to site signals
Choose high points for light signals. If laying out marks on the ground, use level ground or ensure they are on slopes that are not likely to be overlooked in the normal pattern of aerial search. Planes usually fly over hilly territory from the lower to the higher ridges. This means that slopes behind the ridges may be hidden as the plane approaches. If in doubt, locate your signals near the tops of ridges so they are seen from either direction.

Codes

Once contact has been established, if you cannot speak directly to your rescuers there are internationally recognised codes you can use to communicate and signal your basic needs.

must know

Ground-to-air code
Lay the code symbols out in the open, avoiding steep gullies or ravines. Do not locate them on reverse slopes. On snow, trampled-out symbols will show clearly until the next snowfall. Remember to destroy any signals when rescued. They will go on working long after you have gone.

Ground-to-air signals

The ground-to-air code is an internationally recognised emergency signalling system used to attract the attention of air rescuers. Make the symbols as large and noticeable as possible — the recommended size for each one is 10m (40ft) long and 3m (10ft) wide, with 3m (10ft) between symbols. Use the fluorescent marker panels from your survival pouch, or improvise by laying out pieces of wreckage or digging the signs into the earth. Use rocks, boughs and earth banks to accentuate the marks.

Once contact has been made, a message from the aircraft can be answered with A or Y (affirmative) and N (negative) signals, or Morse code or body signals.

Ground-to-air code

1 Serious injury, immediate casevac (casualty evacuation). (Can also mean 'need doctor'.) **2** Need medical supplies. **3** Need food and water. **4** Negative *(No)*. **5** Affirmative *(Yes)* — *(Y will also be understood)*. **6** All is well. **7** Unable to move on. **8** Am moving on this way. **9** Indicate direction to proceed. **10** Do not understand. **11** Need compass and map. **12** Think safe to land here *(Broken at angles, means 'attempting take-off')*. **13** Need radio/signal lamp/battery. **14** Aircraft badly damaged.

Night signals

If you have a supply of petrol or other inflammable substances, you can make signals that will work at night. Dig or scrape an SOS (or any symbol) in the earth, sand or snow and, when the signal is needed, pour petrol into it and ignite it.

Message signalling

The international Morse code can be transmitted by flashing lights on and off, by a simple heliograph, or by waving a flag or a shirt tied to a stick. Do not rely on memory — always carry a copy of the code.

Heliograph

Use the sun and a reflector to flash light signals. Any shiny object will serve — a polished tin lid, glasses,

Morse code

A · —	G — — ·	M — —	S · · ·	Y — · — —	5 · · · · ·
B — · · ·	H · · · ·	N — ·	T —	Z — — · ·	6 — · · · ·
C — · — ·	I · ·	O — — —	U · · —	1 · — — — —	7 — — · · ·
D — · ·	J · — — —	P · — — ·	V · · · —	2 · · — — —	8 — — — · ·
E ·	K — · —	Q — — · —	W · — —	3 · · · — —	9 — — — — ·
F · · — ·	L · — · ·	R · — ·	X — · · —	4 · · · · —	0 — — — — —

Sending signals

AAAAA* etc = Call sign. *I have a message*
AAA* = End of sentence. *More follows*
Pause = End of word. *More follows*
EEEEE* etc = Error. *Start from last correct word*
AR = End of message

Receiving signals

TTTTT* etc = I am receiving you
K = I am ready. *Start message*
T = Word received
IMI* = Repeat sign. *I do not understand*
R = Message received

Useful words

SOS	· · · — — — · · ·
SEND	· · · | · | — · | — · ·
DOCTOR	— · · | — — — | — · · — · | — · | — — — | · — ·
HELP	· · · · | · | · — · · | · — — ·
INJURY	· · | — · | · — — — | · · — | · — · | — · — —
TRAPPED	— | · — · | · — | · — — · | · — — · | · | — · ·
LOST	· — · · | — — — | · · · | —
WATER	· — — | · — | — | · | · — ·

* *Send as one word. No pauses.*

a piece of foil — but a hand-mirror is best. Long flashes are dashes and quick ones dots. If you do not know Morse code, even random flashes should attract attention. At least learn the code for SOS.

A flash can be seen at a great distance and requires little energy. Sweep the horizon during the day. If a plane approaches, make intermittent flashes or you may dazzle the pilot. Once you are certain you have been seen, stop signalling.

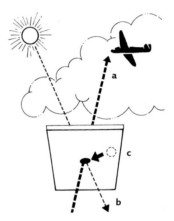

Single-sided reflector: With this improvised reflector, pick up sunlight to get an image on the ground or some other surface and lead it in the direction of the aircraft.

Double-sided reflector: Punch a hole in a double-sided reflector to improvise a heliograph. Sight the target you wish to contact through the hole in the heliograph (a) in the direction of the sun, so the sun shines through the hole (b). You will see a spot of light on your face (c). Angle the mirror so the dot of light on your face 'disappears' back through the hole in the mirror — still sighting your contact.

Rag signals

Tie a flag or a piece of brightly coloured clothing to a pole and move it left for dashes and right for dots. Exaggerate each signal with a figure-of-eight movement (at close range this may not be needed). Keep 'dash' pauses on the left slightly longer than 'dot' movements to the right.

Rag signals: For a 'dot', swing to the right and make a figure-of-eight. For a 'dash', swing to the left and make a figure-of-eight.

Body signals

These signals can be used to send a message to airmen. Note the changes from frontal to sideways positions and the use of leg and body posture as well as hand movements. Use a cloth in the hand to emphasize the 'yes' and 'no' signals. Make all signals in a clear and exaggerated manner.

Body signals

1 Pick us up.
2 Need mechanical help.
3 Land here.
4 Yes.
5 No.
6 All is well.
7 Can proceed shortly.
8 Have radio.
9 Do not attempt to land here.
10 Need medical assistance.
11 Use drop message.

These sound, light and pyrotechnic codes are recognised internationally by mountain rescue services:

- **Message: SOS**
  Flare signal: Red
  Sound signal: 3 short blasts, 3 long, 3 short
  Repeat after 1 minute interval
  Light signal: 3 short flashes, 3 long, 3 short
  Repeat after 1 minute interval
- **Message: Help needed**
  Flare signal: Red
  Sound signal: 6 blasts in quick succession
  Repeat after 1 minute interval
  Light signal: 6 flashes in quick succession
  Repeat after 1 minute interval
- **Message: Message understood**
  Flare signal: White
  Sound signal: 3 blasts in quick succession
  Repeat after 1 minute interval
  Light signal: 3 flashes in quick succession
  Repeat after 1 minute interval
- **Message: Return to base**
  Flare signal: Green
  Sound signal: Prolonged succession of blasts
  Light signal: Prolonged succession of flashes

Pilots will respond to body signals as follows:

- **Message received and understood:**
  In daylight: tipping the plane's wings from side to side. At night: flashing green lights.
- **Message received but not understood:**
  In daylight: flying the plane in a right-handed circle. At night: flashing red lights.

Flares

Any flare will be investigated during a search, but help your rescuers by choosing a colour best fitted to the location. In closely-wooded country, green does not stand out but red does. Over snow, white merges — green and red are best.

Types of flare

Some flares are hand-held and reversible. One end produces smoke for daytime use, the other a flare for use at night. The higher these are held the easier they are to see. Flares and rockets that fire into the air are visible for a greater distance. One type reaches a height of 90m (300ft), where a parachute opens holding the flare suspended for several minutes. Other rockets produce a loud bang and colour balls.

Handling flares

Hand-held flares are cylindrical tubes with a cap at each end. The top cap is often embossed with a letter or pattern so that it can be identified by touch in the dark. Remove it first. Then remove the base cap to expose a short string and a safety pin, or other safety device. Point the flare upwards and away from you or anyone else. Remove the pin, or turn to the fire position. Hold the flare at arm's length, at shoulder height, pointing directly upwards. Sharply pull the firing string vertically downwards and brace yourself for the kickback. Some flares have a spring-mechanism trigger.

Moving on

If you decide that rescue is unlikely and that the best plan is to make your own way back, leave clear signs behind to help rescuers follow your trail. On your way, stay close to regular flight routes or keep to open territory.

Direction markers

These are signals to leave behind if you abandon camp. At the camp leave written messages in containers detailing your plans. Hang them from tripods or trees and draw attention to them with markers. Then make a large arrow shape to indicate the direction in which you have set off that will be visible from the air, and other direction markers which can be interpreted at ground level. Continue to make signals as you proceed. This is useful not only for people to follow but to establish your own route if you start going back on your trail.

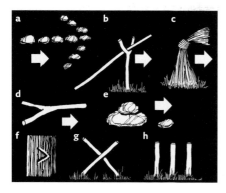

Direction markers could include: rocks or debris placed in an arrow shape (a); a stick in a crooked support, the top indicating the direction followed (b); grasses tied in an overhand knot with the ends hanging in the direction followed (c); forked branches with the fork pointing in the direction followed (d); small rocks set upon larger rocks, with a small rock beside them (e); arrowhead-shape notches cut in tree trunks (f). A cross of sticks or stones means 'not this way' (g). A signal of three sticks or stones means danger or emergency (h).

Search

If you go missing, your intended route — if known by rescue authorities — will form the basis of a search. Most searches follow recognised search patterns. Learn them so you can anticipate how a search party will comb an area looking for you, which in turn will help in timing your distress signals.

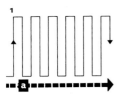

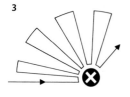

Search patterns

Searches follow recognisable patterns but also take into account your probable strategy, given the terrain and weather conditions.

Searches on the ground
The first search will usually be made on foot along the route you were supposed to have taken.

▶ **A base line search** (1) is carried out when there has been a high wind or bad weather conditions on your known route (a). Searchers deduce that you may have veered from the route to the lee side of a slope for shelter.

▶ **A watercourse search** (2) takes in all the tributaries, using the main stream as a base line. This is undertaken when your last known position was on or near a river.

▶ **A fan search** (3) is used when your last known position (x) is fairly certain but it is impossible to deduce the direction you may have taken.

Aerial searches
If your route has been checked on the ground, rescuers will extend the search to cover the surrounding area. Search patterns from the air cover

both sides of your known route. A night search across a broad area is often made to check for lights.

▶ **A creeping line search** (4), beginning in a corner of the search area, is particularly useful when only a single aircraft is available. It follows parallels running towards and away from the sun so that any reflection from wreckage and signals will be more easily seen.

▶ **A track crawl** (5) covers both sides of the expected route taken (a). The pattern is reversed after flying for one hour.

▶ **A square search** (6) is useful when a comparatively small area is to be covered. The search starts in the last known location (x) and works outwards. If unsuccessful the search is repeated in the other direction.

▶ **A contour search** (7), following the contours as shown, ensures that mountains are searched with maximum thoroughness. Steep valleys are usually searched several times by flying along them.

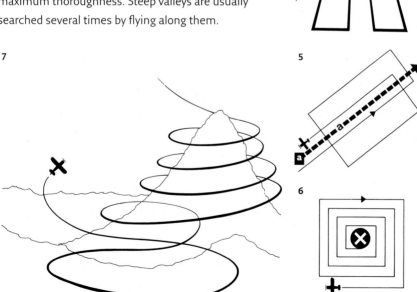

Helicopter rescue

Helicopters are frequently used to carry out rescues. While awaiting rescue, look for a suitable landing site and create one if necessary. If landing is impossible, a rescue may involve winching you from the ground while the helicopter hovers.

Selecting a landing site

A helicopter requires an obstruction-free approach and exit path, both into the prevailing wind. The ground should be level. The touch-down surface should be firm, even and free of loose materials.

Look for a natural clearing. In close country, a river bank on a large bend is often the best natural landing place. Alternatively, climb a spur and select a level piece of ground free of large trees. In mountains, updraughts and downdraughts can be considerable. Select a site that gives maximum lift in the take-off direction.

Preparing a landing site

▶ A level cleared area is needed, at least 26m (80ft) in diameter. A further 5m (15ft) is needed all around, cleared to a height of 60cm (2ft). There should be an approach path into the prevailing wind with no obstructions within an angle of 15 degrees of the central landing pad.

▶ Mark the touchdown point with an H. Use inlaid rocks (keeping the surface smooth) or panel markers. Trample down snow to stop it swirling. In dry areas, water the surface to keep dust down.

▶ Indicate the direction and strength of the wind at the landing place so the pilot can select the best approach. Smoke is an ideal indicator, but do not place it so that it obscures the touchdown area. If a fire is not practical, make a T-sign from contrasting material and place it at the downwind edge of the landing place with the horizontal bar of the T placed upwind. Alternatively, a person standing in the same place with their arms outstretched and back to the wind will suffice.

▶ For a night rescue, have flares and fires prepared to indicate your position once the helicopter is within range. Shine torches or vehicle headlights skyward to attract attention. Once the pilot has seen you, keep the beams low so they do not dazzle him. Shine them on the touchdown area.

Non-landing rescue

If a landing place is out of the question, you can be lifted from the ground while the helicopter hovers.

Winching techniques

A double lift is the usual method but a single lift is sometimes used. Both techniques are suitable for rescue on land or on water. If on water, stow sails, remove your lifeline and stream the sea anchor first.

▶ **Double lift**: A crewman is lowered on the winch with another strop for the survivor. During the lift, the crewman supports the survivor with his legs and hands. Once the strop has been put in place and tightened, do not lift your arms: keep them by your sides.

▶ **Single lift**: This time you fit yourself into the strop. Allow the winch sling to touch down before you approach it to avoid receiving a shock from static electricity. When you have placed it under your armpits and securely tightened the grommet, give the 'thumbs up' sign. Once acknowledged, make no further signals until aboard the chopper — if you raise your arms you risk slipping out of the strop. When you reach the cabin doorway, do exactly as the winchman directs.

Helicopter safety precautions

▶ Never approach a helicopter from the rear: this is a blind spot for the crew and the tail rotor is unprotected.
▶ On sloping ground always approach the helicopter up the slope; never approach down a slope.
▶ Do not carry anything that could foul the main rotor.
▶ Keep sharp objects away from the body panels of the helicopter.
▶ Sit in the seat allocated to you by the crewman, fasten the seat belt and keep it fastened until told otherwise.

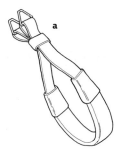

Rescue strop: the strop is connected to the winch hook. Put head and arms through the strop and tighten to fit your chest under your armpits, by sliding the adjusting ring (a).

Rescue at sea

While awaiting rescue at sea, exploit any possibilities of obtaining food from the sea and collecting drinking water. If signalling fails to attract help, head for land or the nearest shipping lane. If you have to make a landfall on a difficult coast, you should know how to lessen the risks.

must know

Survival at sea priorities
- Protect yourself from exposure to the elements.
- Try to establish your location and the best way of attracting a rescue.
- Ration water supplies and start collecting rain. Do not drink sea water, urine or alcohol.
- Do not eat unless you have sufficient water. Check and stow all rations. Start fishing as soon as possible.

Signalling at sea

Flares, dye markers and movement of any kind are the best ways of attracting attention at sea. If you have no signalling equipment, wave clothing or tarpaulins and churn the water if it is still. At night or in fog, a whistle and torch are useful for making contact with other boats.

Radio transmitter

Some boats carry a radio transmitter. Frequencies are usually preset at 121.5 and 243 megacycles and the range is about 32km (20 miles). Transmit an SOS and your location at frequent intervals.

Sea markers

For use in daytime, these markers release dye into the water. Unless the sea is very rough they will be conspicuous for about three hours.

Flares

Day-and-night flares are particularly useful — one end produces smoke for daytime use. Use flares only when you are sure they will be seen — when a plane is flying towards you, for instance, not when it has gone past. Keep all flares dry and secure.

If you do not have flares, use any shiny reflective surface to send heliograph signals to passing aircraft.

Abandoning ship

If you have to abandon your craft, take as much equipment with you as possible, including lifejackets and lifebelts. If possible, put on warm, woollen clothing, including hat and gloves, and wrap a towel around your neck to protect you from exposure to sun and cold. Take a torch if you can, and grab chocolates and boiled sweets if handy.

Inflating a dinghy

Many boats are equipped with dinghy-type lifeboats. Some of these are self-inflating on immersion in salt water. Others come with a pump. There are several inflation points so if one compartment is punctured the others will keep the dinghy afloat. Ensure that the dingy is fully inflated: it should be firm, not rock-hard. Check for leaks. Escaping air will cause bubbles under water or a hissing sound above water. Use conical plugs from the dinghy kit to seal any leaks. If you suspect a leak on the underside, swim below and insert a plug.

Boarding a dinghy

To board a dinghy, place one leg over the edge and roll inside. Do not jump into a dinghy from above: you may damage it. To haul someone else aboard, hold their shoulders and lift one leg over the end, then roll them in. Discourage them from putting their arms around your neck: they could pull you into the water. Once aboard, tie yourself and others to the dinghy, stow all gear in stowage places and tie securely.

Righting a dinghy

Most dinghies have righting straps on the bottom, and larger ones have a righting line attached to one side. Grab it from the opposite side, brace your feet against the dinghy and pull. The dinghy should rise up and over, pulling you out of the water momentarily. In heavy seas this can be difficult.

must know

In rough water
Stream out the sea anchor from the bow: it will keep the front of the boat pointing into the wind and prevent capsizing. Keep low in the craft. Do not sit on the sides or stand up, and never make sudden movements.

Moving on

If an SOS has been successfully sent giving your position, or you know you are in or near regular shipping lanes, it is usually preferable to stay in the same vicinity for 72 hours. Try to maintain location by putting out a sea anchor.

If your signalling has not been successful, move on quickly to take advantage of initial fitness and energy, especially if land is known to be near and downwind. If there is no land nearby, head for the nearest shipping lane.

Your craft will move with the wind and current. In the open ocean, currents seldom exceed a speed of 9-13km (6-8 miles) per day. Use the wind if you can: improvise a sail if you do not have one. Hold the bottom of the sail rather than securing it so you can let go if a gust of wind threatens to capsize the craft. If the wind is against your chosen direction, stream out the sea anchor to maintain position.

Man overboard!

If you are swept overboard, attract attention as quickly as possible. Sound travels well on water and movement will make you more noticeable, so shout and splash, and wave with one arm. If you are wearing a lifejacket it will probably be equipped with a whistle and a light.

Swimming

Swim slowly and steadily. If abandoning a sinking boat, get upwind and stay clear of it. Once clear, look out for a boat or wreckage which can offer support. If there is no boat or dinghy, grab as much flotsam as possible to use as a raft. Tie it together with anything available — ties, belts, shoelaces, clothing. Salvage any floating equipment.

If within sight of land, do not battle against an ebbing tide. Relax and float until it turns and helps to carry you to land. If the sea is too rough to float on your back, adopt this technique:

1 Float upright in the water and take a deep breath.
2 Lower your face into the water (keeping mouth closed) and bring your arms forward to rest at water level.
3 Relax in this position until you need to take in more air.
4 Raise your head above the surface, treading water, and exhale. Take another breath and return to the relaxed head-down position.

Making a landfall

When approaching land, aim for a landing point where it is easy to beach or where you can safely swim ashore. Take down the sail and watch for rocks. The sea anchor will keep you pointing at the shore and slow your progress, allowing you more time to steer clear of rocks.

A sloping beach with a small surf is ideal. If you can time it right, ride in on the back of a breaker. To avoid being swamped or turned sideways by a wave approaching from behind, paddle hard without overshooting the breaker which is carrying you along. In heavy surf, turn the vessel to face seaward and paddle into the wave as it approaches. If you reach land at night, wait until morning to beach if you can — there are too many dangers you can fail to spot in the dark. If you float into an estuary, be sure to reach a bank. The turning tide could carry you back out to sea.

want to know more?

Take it to the next level...
▶ **For more on lighting fires 48-52**
▶ **For more on marker panels and flares in survival equipment 29-30**
▶ **For more on collecting water 62-7**
▶ **For more on sea dangers 111, 119, 126-9**

Other sources...
▶ **Contact local rescue authorities to check their search procedures in advance of your visit. Lodge information with them about your schedule and route.**

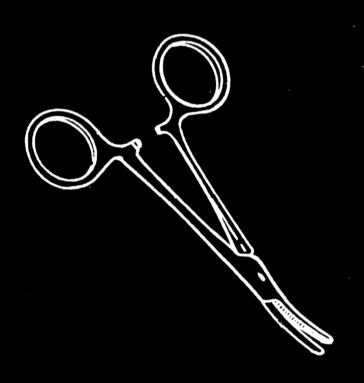

7 First aid

First aid involves attending to injuries and coping with sickness until full medical treatment is available. In some cases, drastic measures may have to be taken before help can arrive in order to save a life. Some of the advice given in this chapter is intended only for such extreme circumstances. Ideally you should have a trained first-aider present.

First aid basics

However careful you are, injuries or illness may occur. First aid skills are essential and everyone in the group should have them. An ability to improvise where medical equipment is not available is an important survival skill.

Unconscious

If someone is breathing but unconscious and does not have a spinal injury, check there are no obstructions in the mouth and the airway is clear, deal with any serious bleeding and place him or her in the recovery position. Check for injury and external bleeding, and try to establish the cause of unconsciousness.

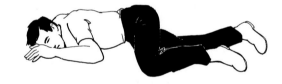

Recovery position: Move the arm and leg on one side outwards to stop the patient lying flat; the elbow and knee should both be bent. Turn the head in the same direction. Lay the other arm down along the side of the patient. Pull the jaw forward and check the tongue is forward, not blocking the airway. Loosen any tight clothing.

Restoring breathing and heartbeat

If the injured person is not breathing, begin artificial respiration immediately. If you cannot feel a pulse, start cardiac compression (external heart massage) while artificial respiration is continued.

Obstructed breathing

Noisy breathing, froth around the nose or lips and blueness around the lips and ears are all signs of obstructed breathing. Check breathing regularly by listening carefully near the nose and mouth. Remove any obstructions in the airway. Check at the neck or wrist for a pulse.

Not breathing

This emergency may be caused by:

▶ Choking

▶ Blockage of upper air passages caused by face and neck injuries or foreign bodies

▶ Drowning or electric shock

▶ Inflammation and spasm of air passages caused by inhalation of smoke, gases or flame

▶ Lack of oxygen

▶ Compression of the chest

Choking and blockages

If breathing has stopped, remove any obstruction in the airway and give artificial respiration. Sweep inside the mouth with a finger and ensure the tongue has not fallen back to obstruct the breathing passages.

If someone appears to be choking, but can breathe and cough, their own coughing is more effective than your aid. A blow on the back may sometimes help. If the victim cannot clear the airway, use the Heimlich manoeuvre.

▶ **Heimlich manoeuvre:** Use this technique if the casualty is conscious.

1 Stand or kneel behind the patient with your arms around them.

must know

Spinal injury
Do not place a casualty with a suspected spinal injury in the recovery position. Use an artificial airway, if available, to maintain respiration.

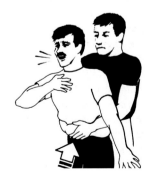

Self-help

If alone, use the Heimlich manoeuvre by pulling on yourself or pushing against a blunt projection, e.g. an earth bank or a fallen tree.

2 Make a fist of one hand and press it, thumb-side inwards, above the patient's navel but below the breastbone. Clasp the other hand round the fist.
3 Pull sharply upwards and inwards four times.
4 If this does not work, give four sharp blows to the back between the shoulderblades and four more 'hugs'.
5 Repeat if the first attempt fails. Be ready to give artificial respiration if the blockage is removed but the patient does not start breathing.
▶ **Unconscious and not breathing:** If the patient is unconscious and there is a blockage, lay them on their back with head tilted back. Kneel astride, placing your hands, one on top of the other, with the heels resting above their navel. Make quick thrusts up towards the centre of the ribcage. If the blockage does not shift, roll the patient on to the side and strike four times between the shoulderblades. Repeat as necessary.

Not breathing and no pulse
When breathing has ceased and no pulse can be found, quickly check the cause and respond appropriately as follows:
▶ **Drowning:** The face, especially lips and ears, are livid and congested. There may be a fine froth at the mouth and nostrils, which is blocking the air passage. Do not attempt to remove liquid from the lungs. Begin artificial respiration after removing any obstructions and treat for cardiac arrest if the pulse stops.
▶ **Electrocution:** The heart may stop and muscle spasms may throw the victim some distance. Do not touch the victim until the electric current is off. Give artificial respiration and treat for cardiac arrest, then treat any burns.

▶ **Lightning:** The victim is usually stunned and falls unconscious. They may have electrical burns. Give artificial respiration (prolonged resuscitation may be needed). Treat for cardiac arrest if the pulse stops. Treat any burns.

▶ **Poisoning:** Poisons which enter the lungs or affect the nervous system can produce asphyxia. Give artificial respiration but avoid traces of poison around the mouth. Treat for cardiac arrest if the pulse stops.

▶ **Heart attack:** The patient is suffering severe chest pain, shortness of breath, giddiness, collapse, heavy sweating, irregular pulse and blueness of lips or skin. If breathing fails, give artificial respiration, and cardiac compression if the pulse stops.

Artificial respiration

Begin artificial respiration as soon as the airway has been cleared. Mouth-to-mouth is the fastest and most effective method. If the face is injured, or poison or chemical burns are suspect, use the Silvester technique.

must know

Do not give up!
With any form of resuscitation the first five minutes are probably the most critical but, if breathing does not start, keep artificial respiration up for at least an hour. In a group take turns. Resuscitation techniques have saved the lives of victims of drowning, hypothermia and electrocution after three hours without spontaneous breathing. Regularly check for a heartbeat. If there is no pulse, start cardiac compression while artificial respiration is continued.

Mouth-to-mouth ('Kiss of life')

1 Lie the patient face up, tilt the head back, hold the jaw well open and nostrils closed.

2 Check the mouth and throat are clear of obstruction.

3 Place your mouth over the patient's and exhale. Watch for the chest rising as you blow gently into the patient's lungs (if it does not, the airway may be blocked: turn the patient sideways and thump between the shoulderblades to remove obstruction).

4 Remove your mouth. Take a deep breath while checking that the chest falls automatically. You should feel or hear air returning.

5 Repeat quickly for the first 6 inflations, then at 12 per minute until breathing is restored.

Artificial respiration: with facial injury

The Silvester method is recommended when poisoning or facial injury prevent mouth-to-mouth resuscitation.

1 Lie the casualty face up, raise the shoulders with a folded blanket or clothing, and kneel astride the casualty's head.

2 Place hands flat over the lower ribs and rock forward, pressing steadily downwards. Lift the arms upwards and outwards as far as possible.

3 Repeat rhythmically about 12 times per minute.

4 If there is no improvement, turn the patient sideways and strike briskly between the shoulders to remove any obstruction before resuming the cycle.

Mouth-to-mouth for children

When administering mouth-to mouth to a child, exhale normally instead of blowing into the mouth. The first four inflations should be given as quickly as possible. Note that blowing forcefully into a child's mouth may damage delicate lungs.

Artificial respiration: face down

The Holger Nielson method is recommended for resuscitating a drowning victim if mouth-to-mouth is not possible, or if the patient cannot be turned on to their back. The face-down position allows liquids to flow freely from the mouth.

1 Place the patient front-down with head turned to one side, arms bent and forehead resting on hands. Loosen tight clothing, ensure the tongue is forward and the mouth is clear of weed, mud, etc.

2 Face the casualty, kneeling at the head. Place your hands over the shoulderblades, with thumbs touching and fingers spread.

3 Perform the following procedure to a count of eight:

1-2-3 Rock forward with arms straight, producing gentle, even, increasing pressure (2 seconds).

4 Rock back, sliding your hands to grasp the patient's upper arms (0.5–1 second).

5-6-7 Raise the patient's arms gently by rocking further backwards (2 seconds). Do not raise the patient's trunk or disturb the head too much.

8 Lower the arms to the ground and slide your hands back to the initial position (0.5–1 second).

4 Repeat 12 times per minute.

If the patient's arms are injured, place a folded garment under the forehead and lift under the armpits. This is not a practicable method if ribs or shoulders are badly damaged.

must know

After breathing is restored
Place the patient in the recovery position after resuscitation. But not in cases of spinal injury.

Is the heart beating?

In a relaxed adult, a normal pulse is 60–80 beats per minute (average 72). In young children it is 90–140 per minute. Excitement increases the rate.

Taking a pulse at the wrist

Rest your fingers lightly at the front of the wrist, over the radial artery, about 1cm (0.3in) from the thumb side at the lower end of the forearm.

Taking a pulse at the neck

Turn the patient's face to one side. Slide your fingers from the Adam's apple into the groove alongside and press gently.

If there is no pulse

If you cannot feel a pulse after 10–12 lung inflations through artificial respiration, and the pupils of the eyes are much larger than normal, start cardiac compression while artificial respiration is continued. The mouth-to-mouth and the Silvester methods can be carried out at the same time.

Cardiac compression

Treat for cardiac arrest as follows:

1 Act swiftly. Place the casualty on a firm surface, chest up.

2 Using the edge of your hand, strike firmly on the lower part of the breastbone (sternum) — the central bone between the ribs. The jarring may start the heart.

3 If there is still no pulse proceed with compression. Kneel beside the casualty. Place the heel of one hand on the lower half of the breastbone. Make sure

must know

When a pulse returns
Stop cardiac compression as soon as a pulse returns. Never give compression if the heart is beating — even if only a very faint pulse can be felt. You could stop the heart.

it is not on the end of, or below, the breastbone. Place heel of the other hand over it (keeping rest of hand off the chest). With arms straight, rock forward and press down 6–8 times after each lung inflation.

4 As soon as a pulse is detected, stop compressions but continue inflations until the casualty is breathing unaided. Place the victim in the recovery position (unless spine or neck injured).

Adults: Press down about 4cm (1.5in). Repeat at least 60 times per minute. Press smoothly and firmly. Erratic or rough pressing could cause further injury.

Infants and children: Require less pressure and more pushes. For babies and small children, light pressure with two fingers is enough at a rate of 100 times per minute. For children up to ten years, use the heel of one hand only and push 80–90 times per minute.

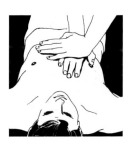

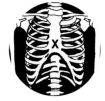

Bleeding

An average person has up to 6·25 litres (11pt) of circulating blood. The loss of 0·5 litre (1pt) causes mild faintness, 1 litre (2pt) faintness with an increase in pulse and breathing, 1·5 litres (3pt) collapse. More than 2.24 litres (4pt) may cause death.

must know

Bleeding and not breathing
Blood transports life-giving oxygen. When bleeding is coupled with cessation of breathing, treat both together as a double emergency.

Bleeding from veins and capillaries

This usually can be stopped by applying pressure directly over the bleeding point.

1 Squeeze the edges of a gaping wound together.

2 Use a sterile dressing to apply pressure, or a clean, non-fluffy cloth. As a last resort, use your hand to prevent blood loss. If unsure of the exact point of haemorrhage, use a large pad over a wide area. Maintain pressure for 5–10 minutes to allow clotting to take place.

3 If the wound is on a limb, raise it above the level of the heart; if broken, do not elevate the limb until it has been properly splinted.

Arterial bleeding

Act quickly to stop blood spurting from an artery. Control the bleeding by applying pressure to a pressure point — where the artery runs near the surface over a bone.

1 Apply pressure to the pressure point using your fingers, thumb or heel of the hand. At the same time apply direct pressure to the wound and elevate extremities.

2 When bleeding is under control, apply a sterile dressing and bandage (not so tight as to cut off circulation).

3 Do not lift the dressing — if a clot is disturbed the bleeding will be made worse.

Guarding against infection

Infectious diseases, including HIV and hepatitis, are transmitted via the exchange of bodily fluids. Do not touch open wounds with your fingers unless absolutely necessary. If possible, place a barrier between you and the victim's blood or body fluids, using a thin piece of plastic, rubber gloves or a clean cloth. Wash your hands with soap and warm water before and after providing care.

Pressure points

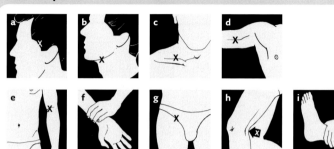

The pictures show where to apply pressure to staunch arterial blood loss from the areas specified.

Pressure point	Blood loss area
Forward of/above ear (a)	Temple or scalp
Side of jaw (b)	Face below eyes
Above clavicle (c)	Shoulder or upper arm
Underside of upper arm (d)	Elbow
Crook of elbow (e)	Lower arm
Front of wrist (f)	Hand
Midway on groin/top of thigh (g)	Thigh
Upper sides of knee (h)	Lower leg
Front of ankle (i)	Foot

Internal bleeding

This serious condition is common after a violent blow to the body, broken bones, bullet or deep penetration wounds. Internal bleeding may occur if an organ such as a kidney, liver or spleen has been damaged.

1 For serious internal bleeding, the only treatment is specialised nursing care. Seek medical help.

2 Monitor airway, breathing and circulation.

3 Lie the patient flat with legs elevated. Maintain a moderate body temperature.

4 Treat for shock. Reassure casualty.

5 For bruising, apply ice or cold pack, with cloth to prevent damage to skin.

Nose bleed

Sit the patient up with head slightly forward and pinch the soft part of the nostrils for five minutes. Encourage the patient to breathe through the mouth, and not to sniff, rub or blow the nose. Loosen tight clothing. If the patient loses consciousness, place them on their side to allow blood to drain from the nose. Seek professional medical help.

Internal bleeding symptoms

Initially there may be little evidence of internal injury, perhaps only slight bruising under the skin. The patient will feel light-headed, restless and faint, and look pale with cold and clammy skin, with a weak pulse. Subsequent signs of internal bleeding include:

Symptom	Source of haemorrhaging
Red or wine colouring to urine	Kidneys or bladder
Blood passed with faeces	Lower bowel
Partly digested blood gives black tarry appearance to faeces	Upper bowel
Blood vomited — bright red	Stomach — fresh bleeding
Blood vomited — like brown coffee grounds	Stomach — not recent bleeding
Coughed up blood, frequently as red froth	Lungs

---

must know

Cleaning wounds
Use boiled water and soap to wash and scrub your hands first. Wash the wound in (cooled) boiled water or if none is available use urine, which is sterile and will not introduce infection.

must know

Use of antiseptics
If antiseptic is available use it for cuts and abrasions. Do not use antiseptics on deep wounds as they cause further tissue drainage.

Wounds

Open wounds are at risk of infection by bacteria, especially tetanus (immunisation is advisable for all trips). Clean a wound and dress it as follows:

1 Cut away the clothing from the wound site, clean the vicinity using (cooled) boiled water and irrigate the wound to wash out the dirt. Clean the wound from the centre outwards. Then dry.

2 Remove any foreign bodies. This is best left for a trained medic, but in a survival situation you may need to do it yourself. Use sterile tweezers and clean the wound thoroughly afterwards.

3 Apply a clean dressing.

4 Immobilise the wound in a comfortable position.

5 Change the dressing if it becomes wet, omits an offensive smell, or if pain in the wound increases and throbs, indicating infection.

Infected wounds

Soak the infected area in hot salty water, or apply a poultice to draw out the pus and reduce swelling.

Clay or anything that can be mashed can be used as a poultice, for example rice, potatoes, roots or shredded tree bark. Boil, wrap in a cloth and apply the poultice to the infected area as hot as can be tolerated. Applied heat, for example a warm rock wrapped in a cloth, can also aid healing.

Open treatment
The safest way to manage most wounds is to cover them with a dressing but not to suture. If the wound is difficult to clean, leaving it open allows it to heal. Deep wounds may have to be drained. When lancing a wound, sterilise the knife blade first.

Stitching wounds
Clean the wound thoroughly, then stitch across it, or use butterfly sutures from your survival kit for minor wounds (sutures can be applied without any special skills). If the wound becomes infected — red, swollen, tense — remove some or all the stitches to let pus out. Leave to drain.

Stitches: Use a sterilised needle and thread or gut. Make each stitch individually, beginning across the mid-point of the wound. Draw the edges together and tie off the thread.

Adhesive sutures: Use butterfly sutures or cut adhesive plasters in a butterfly shape. Draw the edges of the wound together and apply the plaster across the wound.

Treatment of wounds

Chest wound: If the chest cavity is penetrated, air is sucked into the wound as the patient breathes, which can cause collapse of the lungs. Place the palm of your hand over the wound to prevent air entering. Lay the casualty down, head and shoulders supported, inclining to the injured side. Plug the wound with a large, loose wet dressing, or cover it with a plastic film or aluminium foil (ideally coated with petroleum jelly). Bandage firmly.

Abdominal wounds: No solids or liquid must be given. Relieve thirst by using a damp cloth to moisten the lips and tongue of the patient. If the gut is extruded, cover and keep it damp. Do not attempt to push it back into place. If no organs extrude, dress and bandage firmly.

Head injuries: Ensure the airway is maintained and the tongue is forward. Remove any false or detached teeth. Control any bleeding. If no neck or spinal injuries, place an unconscious patient in the recovery position.

Burns

Remove clothes
Remove smouldering clothes at once from a burn victim as they retain heat and can be hotter than the flames themselves.

Burns cause severe pain and fluid loss. Victims are susceptible to shock. Treat a dry burn as follows:

1 Extinguish burning clothing without fanning the flames. Get the victim down on the ground and roll them over, covering them with a blanket if possible.

2 Remove smouldering clothing and jewellery that may become tighter if swelling occurs.

3 Drench the burned tissues with water to cool them. Ideally, submerge under slow-running cold water for at least 10 minutes.

Types of burn

Deep burns are charred or white in appearance, possibly with bone and muscle visible. Superficial burns are much more painful and may cause greater shock than deep burns.

Burn	Cause	Treatment
Scalds	Hot liquids	Treat as for dry burns.
Mouth and throat	Inhaling flame or hot gases; drinking from a very hot vessel; swallowing boiling liquids or corrosive chemicals	Give sips of cold water to cool. Swelling in the throat may affect breathing — artificial respiration may be required.
Eye	Spitting fat or corrosive chemicals	Hold the eyelid open and pour plenty of water over it to wash out chemicals. Tilt the head so that chemical is not washed into the mouth or nose or into the other eye.
Chemical	Accidental spillage	Use copious amounts of water to dilute and wash off chemicals. Remove clothing that may retain corrosive substances. Do not try to neutralise acid with alkali or vice-versa. Treat as for dry burns.
Electrical and lightning	Exposure to faulty cabling or storm lightning	Give artificial respiration if necessary. Treat as for dry burns. Take no risks if current still live.

4 Do not apply antiseptic, butter or ointments. Continue cooling until withdrawal from water does not lead to increase in pain.

5 Apply dry, sterile dressings to burns.

6 Later, hardwood barks such as oak or beech, which contain tannin, can be boiled in water, cooled, and applied to burnt flesh to soothe the wound.

7 Give the patient fluids in the form of small cold drinks with half a teaspoonful of salt or bicarbonate of soda to a pint of water.

must know

Burns and shock
Most burns will result in shock. Flooding extensive burns with cold water could increase shock, but that must be weighed against reducing damage to tissues.

Fractures

There are two types of fracture: open and closed. In an open fracture the bone may push through the skin and infection can gain direct access to the bone. A closed fracture does not penetrate the skin.

Without touching or moving the casualty, examine for fractures before swelling complicates the task of locating broken bones. If you have to move the patient, immobilise them first.

Reduction

If medical help is expected, immobilise any closed fractures and leave them for professional treatment. If no help is expected soon, reduce closed fractures as early as possible after injury by applying traction (a slow, strong pull until the edges of the fractured bone are brought together). Check alignment, then splint and immobilise the limb. For the splint, use ski sticks, branches, driftwood, rolls of newspaper, etc. To avoid pressure sores, the splint should be separated from the skin by padding — moss is useful for this. Do not tie splints directly over the injury or allow knots to press against the limb.

Sling materials
Triangular bandages make good slings and supports, or improvise from pieces of clothing, belts, etc.

Immobilisation

Immobilise the whole length of the limb. Use slings to support bent-arm fractures. If no splint is available, or to increase immobilisation, strap the injured limb to the body. Insert padding to keep limbs in position. Use soft material to secure firmly above and below the fracture and below the nearest joints. Place all knots on the same side, giving easy access.

Fracture of arm below elbow (1)

Place the sling (e.g. a sweater) between the arm and the body. Immobilise from the elbow to mid-fingers with a padded splint (a). Take one arm of the sweater behind the head and tie to the other arm on the opposite side (b). Knot below the elbow to stop slipping. Elevating the arm prevents it from swelling.

Fracture at elbow (2)

If the elbow is bent, support it in a narrow sling (a). Bind across the upper arm and chest to prevent movement. Check the pulse to ensure that an artery is not trapped. If the elbow is straight, do not bend it (b). Place a pad in the armpit and strap the arm to the body or place padded splints either side of the arm for support.

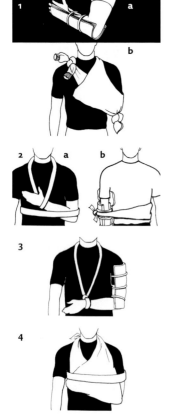

Fracture of upper arm (3)

Place a pad in the armpit with a splint from shoulder to elbow on the outside of the arm and a narrow sling at the wrist. Bind the arm to the chest.

Fracture of shoulderblade or collarbone (4)

Make a sling to take the weight off the injured part. Immobilise with a bandage across the arm and body.

Fracture of hip or upper leg (5)

Place a splint on the inside leg and another from ankle to armpit (a). Use a stick to push tying bands under the hollows of the injured leg. If no splints are available, pad a folded blanket between the legs and tie the broken leg to the sound leg (b).

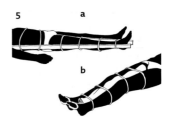

Fracture to knee (6)

If the leg is straight, place the splint behind it (a). Apply a cold compress to the knee (ice if possible). If the leg is bent, bring both legs together, place padding between the calves and thighs, and strap (b). This is a temporary measure until medical help is available. If rescue is unlikely, or a long time away, the leg must be made as straight as possible.

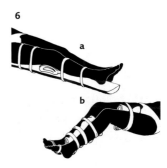

Fracture to lower leg (7)

Splint from above the knee to beyond the heel, or pad between the legs and tie them together.

Fracture of ankle or foot (8)

This is not usual to splint. Elevate the foot to reduce swelling. Immobilise with a folded blanket strapped twice at the ankle and once under the foot. If this is a closed fracture (no wound), leave the shoe on to provide stability. Do not put weight on the foot.

Fracture of pelvis (9)

Place padding between the legs. Bandage around the feet, ankles and knees, with two overlapping bandages over the pelvis (a). Or pad between the thighs, tie at the knees and ankles, place a pillow beneath bent legs and strap the casualty to a flat support at shoulder, waist and ankle (b).

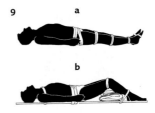

must know

Check circulation
Once a limb has been immobilised, check circulation periodically. Blue or ashen fingers and toes are the obvious warning signs that straps and dressings are too tight.

Fracture of the skull

Symptoms include blood or straw-coloured fluid seeping from the ear or nose. Place the casualty in the recovery position, with the leaking side down. Check breathing and pulse. Completely immobilise.

Fracture of the spine

Symptoms include pain in the back or neck, with possible loss of sensation in the lower limbs. Test for 'feeling' by gently touching a limb. Ask the casualty to move fingers and toes. Immobilise by placing solid objects to prevent movement of head or body.

Fracture of the neck

Immobilise the whole body. Use a cervical collar or place a bag of earth or similar against either side of the neck to prevent movement.

Make a cervical collar from rolled-up newspaper, a folded towel, a car mat, etc. Fold to 10-14cm (4-5.5in) wide to fit from the top of the breastbone to the jaw. Fold in the edges to make it narrower at the back than the front. Overlap around the neck and secure with a belt or tie.

Sprains

A sprain is caused by the wrenching or tearing of tissues connected to the joint. The symptoms are pain and swelling. Sprains are best exercised through a range of movements, but not put under painful stress or you risk permanent damage.

must know

Sprain or fracture?
If in doubt about whether an injury is a sprain or a break, treat it as a fracture.

Bathe the joint with cold water to reduce swelling.
Support with a non-constricting bandage — crepe if
possible. Elevate the affected limb and rest.

Dislocations

A fall, blow or sudden force applied to a joint can
cause a dislocation. Symptoms include pain and
deformity, often with one end of the bone clearly felt
under the skin (there is no grating sound as the
bone ends are not usually damaged). Muscle spasms
fix the bone in position, making it painful to replace.
Shoulders are especially prone to dislocation.

Treating dislocation

▶ **Dislocated shoulder:** Take off your shoe and put
your foot in the patient's armpit, then pull on the
arm. Support the arm with a sling and immobilise
with a bandage across the chest.

▶ **Dislocated finger:** The finger should be pulled
then gently released so that the bone slips back into
place. Try only gently with a dislocated thumb. If it
does not work first time, leave it alone.

▶ **Dislocated jaw:** Place a pad of cloth over the
lower teeth. With the patient's head resting on a
firm support, press downwards on the pad with your
thumbs, simultaneously rotating the dislocated side
of the jaw backwards and upwards with your fingers.
It should snap into place. Bandage round the head
and under the jaw. Feed on soft foods.

Shock

Blood loss, burns, abdominal injuries, electrocution
and heart attack commonly lead to shock. In severe
injuries, it can stop the heart.

1 Reassure the casualty and encourage rest. Lay them flat and elevate the legs. Do not move the casualty unnecessarily.

2 Loosen tight or restrictive clothing around the neck, chest or abdomen. Do not give liquids. Maintain body heat but do not add heat.

3 If breathing or the heart stops, give mouth-to-mouth resuscitation and cardiac compression.

4 Treat all injuries and relieve pain with drugs if available. Shock can take a long time to pass.

Bandaging

A triangular bandage, with short sides not less than 1m (3ft), is a versatile dressing for slings and bandages. Crepe roll bandages are used to hold dressings in place and to secure splints. If necessary, you can improvise bandages from all kinds of material, especially clothing.

For areas that are difficult to bandage, adhesive tapes are useful for fixing dressings. Or use them to fix a dressing or bandage to another bandage if the patient is allergic to the adhesive.

Dressings

Before bandaging, apply a dressing — a pad of cotton wool covered with gauze in a sterile wrapping, or improvised from any clean, non-fluffy material. Apply the dressing without touching the pad. Change dressings when they smell or become wet, or when throbbing indicates infection.

Roll bandaging

Bandages should be applied firmly enough to stop slipping, but not so tight as to cut into the flesh or

A triangular bandage can be used in many ways.

interfere with circulation. Roll the bandage and begin bandaging on a diagonal to anchor it. Each turn should overlap the previous one by two-thirds, with the edges parallel. Tuck in the ends below the last layer and secure with a safety pin or adhesive tape, or tie in a reef knot away from the wound.

Moving the injured

Improvise a stretcher by passing two poles through pieces of sacking, heavy plastic bags or clothing, or use a door or table top. If no poles are available, roll in the sides of a blanket and use the rolls to get a firm grip when carrying. Always test an improvised stretcher before using it.

Lifting

A patient can be lifted using the blanket they are lying on. Other ways to lift depend upon the number of helpers. When lifting with several helpers, agree signals first for synchronizing movements.

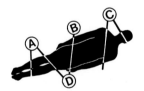

With 4 persons: C supports head and shoulders; D hooks fingers with adjoining hands of B and A to aid lift; A, B and C support while D places the stretcher in position. D helps lower the patient.

With 3 persons: Place the stretcher at the patient's head. C lifts at the knees; A and B lock fingers under shoulders and hips. Move the casualty from the foot of the stretcher to over it.

With 2 persons: Both stand astride casualty. B links arms beneath shoulders; A lifts with one hand under the thighs, the other under the knees. Both move forward to a position above the stretcher.

Lifting on your own

If no help is available, choose a method you can sustain without dropping the patient. If the casualty

Move only if they are in further danger. Three or four people should help to roll the casualty onto a stretcher. One person should be responsible for maintaining stability of the head and neck. Another holds the shoulders. Do not bend or twist the casualty. If working alone, pull the casualty by the shoulders if face down, by the ankles if face up, in the direction in which the body is lying. Do not twist or turn the casualty over. On rough ground, drag from behind, pulling by the shoulders and resting the casualty's head on your forearms.

is too heavy to lift, drag them on a blanket or a coat.

▶ **Cradle:** Suitable for small children or the very lightweight. Lift with one arm beneath the knees, the other around the shoulders.

▶ **Crutch:** Place and hold the casualty's arm around your neck. Put your arm around their waist, grasping their clothing at the hip.

▶ **Pick-a-back:** Crouch while the casualty puts their arms around your neck. Lift their legs on either side of your body. The casualty must be conscious and injuries must permit them to hold on to your shoulders or around your neck.

▶ **Fireman's lift:** This is not a suitable method if the casualty is heavy or has a head or facial injury (the head hangs down).

Fireman's lift (conscious casualty): Grasp the casualty's right wrist. Place your head under their arm and bend so your shoulder is level with the lower abdomen (a). Bend your knees, allowing the weight to fall across your shoulders and back. Place your right arm between or around the legs (b). Transfer the casualty's right wrist to your right hand and lift, taking weight on your right shoulder (c). Stand up and adjust the weight across your shoulders (d).

Unconscious casualty: Place the casualty face down, kneel at the head and slide your hands under their shoulders. Lift them under the armpits to a kneeling position, then to upright. Raise the casualty's right arm (with your left hand). Continue as for conscious casualty.

▶ **Lifting with a sling:** This is the best one-man carry for long distances. Make a sling wide enough not to cut into the casualty and long enough to go over your shoulders and twice across the victim's back. Two triangular bandages or broad belts would suffice. Use padding to prevent cutting or rubbing.

Place the sling under the casualty's thighs and lower back (a). Lie between the casualty's legs and put your arms through the loops. Tighten the slack in the sling. Grasp the casualty's hand and leg on the injured side (b). Roll away from the injured side, turning over so that the casualty lies on top (c). Adjust the sling to make the load comfortable and rise to a kneeling position (d). The belt will lift the casualty on your back. You should be able to proceed with both hands free (e).

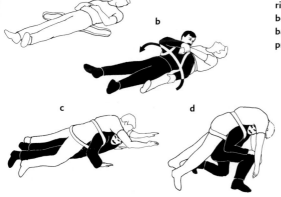

Bites

Infection is the primary risk from animal bites. Rabies, if allowed to develop, is almost always fatal (symptoms are increasing irritability, dislike of light, hydrophobia — a violent aversion to water — and paralysis). Care must be taken not to transmit the disease to anyone else. Bites can also cause tetanus. Anti-tetanus shots are sensible for everyone.

If bitten by a venomous snake or spider, ideally the victim should receive anti-venom within one or two hours. The type of snake or spider must be known so the correct anti-venom can be prepared (see pages 121-5 for illustrations of some of the most venomous snakes and spiders).

must know

Risk of rabies
If you are bitten by an animal, even if the bite heals and all seems well, you must report the bite and be examined by a doctor as soon as possible. If travelling to an area where rabies may be present, have a rabies vaccine before you leave.

How to treat bites and stings

Bite/sting	Treatment
Animal bite	Thoroughly cleanse the bitten area, washing for at least five minutes. Then deal with bleeding, and dress and bandage the wound.
Snake bite	To prevent poison spreading through the body, make the victim relax, wash away any venom on the skin (use soap), place a restricting bandage — to apply firm pressure but not so the limb darkens or swells up — above the bite, and bandage down over the bite. For a bite on the torso, apply pressure with a wad of fabric. Place the wound in a stream of cool water. Treat for shock. Check breathing and administer artificial respiration if needed. Never try to suck out the poison.
Spider bite	Treat as for snake bite. A cold compress helps reduce pain (ice wrapped in cloth is ideal).
Bee sting	Bee stings should be removed from the skin quickly by stroking the sting with the side of a needle, then extracting with tweezers. Do not squeeze the poison sac as this will release more venom. Apply a cold compress.

must know

Avoiding disease
▶ Get immunised before travelling.
▶ Purify drinking water.
▶ Clean hands when preparing or eating food.
▶ Eat a balanced diet.
▶ Wash and peel fruit.
▶ Sterilise eating utensils.
▶ Cover body to reduce risk of insect bites.
▶ Boil water for cleaning teeth.
▶ Cover wounds.
▶ Bury excreta.
▶ Protect food and drink from flies and vermin.
▶ Do not camp near stagnant water and swamps.

Scorpions can inject powerful venom. Bee, wasp and hornet stings can cause severe reactions in some people. Multiple stings are very dangerous — the amount of toxin and the inflammation this causes may affect respiration. Avoid mosquito and other small insect bites by using insect repellent and netting at night.

Diseases

Infectious diseases are caused by bacteria (e.g. cholera, dysentery, tuberculosis), viruses (e.g. colds, 'flu, measles, HIV) and rickettsiae (e.g. typhus). Such contagious diseases are unlikely to occur unless you have brought them with you or catch them from people you meet. On an outdoor trip you are more likely to be exposed to water-borne diseases, or those carried by insects and animals. Where drugs are not available, treatment is largely a matter of dealing with symptoms and making the patient comfortable.

Hot and cold climate hazards

Prickly heat and other warm climate ailments can occur whenever people are exposed to very hot conditions without acclimatisation. Heavy exertion and excessive sweating are often the precipitating factors so take precautions and do not over exert during the hottest part of the day.

Health hazards caused by low temperatures are common not only in the polar regions. Prolonged exposure to cold is dangerous anywhere. Make sure you have adequate clothes, shelter and food.

Warm climate ailments

Ailment	Cause	Symptoms	Treatment
Prickly heat	Sweat glands blocked through heavy sweating and rubbing by clothing.	Uncomfortable skin irritation.	Wash body with cool water. Put on dry clothes. Take antihistamine.
Heat cramp	Lack of salt. Occurs in muscles.	Shallow breathing, vomiting, dizziness.	Rest in shade. Drink water with pinch of salt.
Heat exhaustion	Excessive sweating from heat and humidity.	Palour, cold and clammy skin, weak pulse, dizziness, may become delirious.	As for cramps.
Heatstroke	The most serious result of heat exposure.	Hot dry skin, flushed face, high temperature, fast pulse, severe headache, vomiting. Unconsciousness may follow.	Rest in ventilated, damp shady spot. Sprinkle tepid (not cold) water over body and fan to cool. Drink water. Replace clothing when temperature normal.
Sunburn	Direct sun — a danger especially for pale, sensitive skin.	Burns with blistering. Possibly fatal if over two-thirds of body affected.	Keep in shade. Take pain-killers. Dress blisters and do not burst.
Dehydration	Body fluid loss through excessive sweating.	Thirst, lack of appetite, flushed skin, sleepiness, nausea, delirium, swollen tongue, dim vision.	Take regular sips of water. Rest in a cool place.

Cold climate hazards

Ailment	Cause	Symptoms	Treatment
Hypothermia	Exposure to elements, exhaustion, immersion in cold water.	Low body temperature, irrational and slow responses, shivering, headaches, blurred vision, abdominal pains. Unconsciousness sometimes follows. Can be fatal.	Prevent further heat loss. Replace wet clothing with dry, one garment at a time. Apply warmth to stomach, small of back, armpits, back of neck, wrists, between thighs (use other bodies or hot rocks). Take warm fluids and sugary foods. Wrap in foil blanket.
Frostbite	Extreme cold causing skin and flesh to freeze, especially extremities.	Prickly feeling, waxy, numb patches on skin (later becoming hard and painful), swelling, reddening, blistering. Extremities can deaden and drop off.	If waxy signs, exercise affected area and warm (e.g. under armpits). Deep frostbite: thaw gradually with warm water (28-28·5°C, 108-109°F). Do not burst blisters or rub affected part. Severe pain is an indication that the part has been warmed too quickly.
Snow blindness	Sun or bright reflections from snow or ice causing temporary blindness.	Eyes become sensitive to glare, vision takes on a pink hue, eyes feel gritty.	Get into a dark place and blindfold eyes. Apply cool wet cloth to forehead. Wear goggles and blacken beneath eyes with charcoal to reduce glare.
Trench foot	Feet immersed in water, or damp and cold for a long time. Tight-fitting boots accelerate the condition.	Pins and needles, numbness, sharp pains. Feet appear purple, swollen and blistered.	Dry feet, elevate and keep warm. Do not rub blisters or massage.

Remember: If heat is lost rapidly: rewarm rapidly. If heat is lost slowly: rewarm slowly.

Poisoning

Only induce vomiting in cases of suspected plant poisoning, never if corrosive substances or solvents have been swallowed. Burns around the mouth

indicate a caustic substance is involved. If the skin has been damaged, treat as for burns. Place the victim in the recovery position. If artificial respiration is needed, avoid poison around the mouth. Some plants, such as Poison Ivy, Poison Sumac and Poison Oak, can produce skin irritation. All skin and clothes that have been in contact with the plant should be washed with soap and water.

A universal antidote for poison is made from tea and charcoal, with an equal part of milk of magnesia if available. The poison is absorbed by the charcoal and passes out of the system.

Minor ailments

Even the most minor ailment should not be ignored.

▶ **Blisters:** Reduce the risk of friction blisters by wearing well-fitting shoes and two pairs of socks — an inner pair of nylon and an outer pair of wool. If one occurs:

1 Wash the area of the blister.

2 Pierce the blister near its edge using a sterilised needle. Gently press out the fluid.

3 Cover with a cloth and a tape or a bandage on top.

▶ **Objects in the eye:** Use a mirror if doing this yourself:

1 Pull the lower eyelid downwards to see the inside surface (ask the patient to look upwards). Remove any foreign bodies with a moist corner of cloth.

2 If the problem is under the upper lid, try pulling the lid down over the lower lashes and letting them brush it out.

▶ **Earache:** A result of infection or wax in the eardrum.

1 Warm up a few drops of an edible oil.

2 Pour the oil into the ear and plug with cotton wool.

▶ **Toothache:** Usually caused by an exposed nerve.

1 Plug the cavity with pine-tree resin.

2 If a tooth is knocked out, put a cloth pad on the empty socket and apply pressure to stop bleeding.

want to know more?

Take it to the next level...
▶ For more on tying a bowline knot to make a lifeline 109
▶ For more on camp hygiene and water sterilisation 46-7
▶ For more on identifying venomous snakes and spiders 121-5
▶ For more on soap as an antiseptic 47

Other sources...
▶ Increase your knowledge of first aid by taking a recognised first aid course.
▶ Study natural medicine: medicinal plants can be used when medical supplies are exhausted.
▶ Ask your doctor or tourist office about diseases prevalent in the areas you are visiting and take all necessary precautions.

Further reading

Hunter, Jane and Mears, Ray: *Ray Mears' World of Survival*, Collins, 2003

Mabey, Richard: *Food for Free*, Collins, 2001

Mears, Ray: *Outdoor Survival Handbook*, Ebury Press, 2001

Peter, Libby: *Rock Climbing: Essential Skills & Techniques*, Cordee, 2004

Tippett, Julian: *Navigation for Walkers*, Cordee, 2001

Townsend, Chris: *The Backpacker's Handbook*, Higher Education, 2004

Wilson, Neil: *The SAS Tracking & Navigation Handbook*, Lyons Press, 2001

Wiseman, John "Lofty": *The SAS Urban Survival Handbook*, HarperCollins, 1996

Wiseman, John "Lofty": *The SAS Survival Handbook*, HarperCollins, 2003

Need to Know? First Aid, Collins, 2006

Need to Know? Knots, Collins, 2005

Websites

www.w-o-w.com World Outdoor Web

www.atmagazine.co.uk Adventure Travel Magazine

www.nationalgeographic.com

www.ordnancesurvey.com

www.go4awalk.com

www.countrysideaccess.gov.uk

www.thebmc.co.uk British Mountaineering Council

www.ldwa.org.uk The Long Distance Walkers Association

www.visitbritain.com

www.campingandcaravanningclub.co.uk

www.britishorienteering.org.uk

www.mountainzone.com

www.backpackersclub.co.uk

www.v-g.me.uk Walking and Backpacking in Britain

www.abc-of-hiking.com

www.ukclimbing.com

www.campingmagazine.co.uk

www.out-and-about.co.uk

www.camping.uk-directory.com

www.ukcampsite.co.uk

Index

abseiling 107
alligators 116-17
altimeters 21
angling 87-8
animals
  dangerous 116-29
  food from 81-9
  tracks 81-3
avalanches 130-1
back-packs 17-18
back-up 22
bears 116
camp
  discipline 47
  hygiene 46-7
  where to 36
clothing 16
clouds 101-2
codes
  ground-to-air 148
  Morse 149
  mountain rescue 152
compass 7, 95-6
cooking 54-7
crocodiles 116-17
currents 111-13
dinghy 159-61
direction finding
  compass 7, 95-6
  North pole 93, 98
  shadows 94
  south 98-9
  stars & moon 97-9
  watch 94-5
earthquakes 140-1
emergency plan 20
equipment 16-21, 24-33
fire
  forest 132-3
  fuel 49-50
  lighting a 51-2
  signals 145-6

first aid
artificial respiration
  167-9, 171
bandaging 182-3
bites 185-6
bleeding 171-4
breathing 164-9
burns 176-7
cardiac compression
  170-1
choking 165-6
cold hazards 188
diseases 46, 186
dislocations 181
dressings 182
fractures 177-80
heart attack 167
heat hazards 187
Heimlich manoeuvre
  165-6
immobilisation
  178-80
minor ailments 189
moving injured 183-5
poisoning 72, 188-9
pulse 166-7, 170-1
recovery position
  164
shock 181-2
sprains 180-1
unconscious 164
wounds 174-5
fish & fishing 119, 86-9
flares 30, 152-3
floods 135-6
food
  animals for 81-9
  balanced diet 68-9
  plants for 69-81
  preservation 58-9
  testing plants 70
forest fires 132-3

fungi
  edible 79
  poisonous 80-1
G.P.S. 18
groups
  crossing rivers 112-13
  moving 104-6
  pace 105
  planning 22
  radio discipline 19-20
helicopter rescue 156-7
hurricanes 137-8
igloo 45
insects 85, 117-18,
  121-2
jungle travel 108
kit
  stowing 18
  survival 24-7
  survival pouch 28-31
knives 32-3
knots 40, 87, 109
latrines 46
liferafts 159-61
lightning 134-5
maps 92-3
medicines 27
mobile phones 20
Morse code 149
night walking 106
packs 17-18
planning 21-3
plants
  edibility test 70
  edible 73, 75-6, 77-9
  poisonous 72, 74, 77,
    80
quicksand 110
radios 19
rafts 108-10
rescue 142-61
river, crossing a 110-13

rope making 43
rubbish disposal 46
salt 67
scheduling 22
sea rescue 158-9
search patterns 154-5
sharks 119-20, 129
shelters 36-45
signalling
  body signals 151-2
  direction markers 153
  distress signals 144
  fire signals 145-6
  heliograph 149
  rag signals 150
  transmitters 144-5
signals plan 19
sleeping bags 16-17
snakes 117-18, 123-5
snares 84
SOS 144, 149
spiders 121-2
storms 134-9
survival kit 24-7
survival pouch 28-31
tides 111
tornadoes 138-9
trapping 84
tsunamis 140-1
upland travel 106-8
vaccinations 15
vehicles 21
ventilation 37, 39
water creatures 126-9,
  119
water, drinking
  finding 62
  collection 63-7
  making safe 27, 47,
    64-6
waterways 108-13
weather 100-3

☼ Collins need to know?

Look out for these recent titles in Collins' practical and accessible need to know? series.

  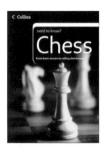 

Other titles in the series:

Antique Marks	Dog Training	Poker	The World
Birdwatching	Drawing & Sketching	Pregnancy	Yoga
Body Language	Dreams	Property	Zodiac Types
Buying Property in France	Golf	Speak French	
Buying Property in Spain	Guitar	Speak Italian	
Card Games	How to Lose Weight	Speak Spanish	
Children's Parties	Kama Sutra	Stargazing	
Codes & Ciphers	Kings and Queens	Watercolour	
Decorating	Knots	Weddings	
Digital Photography	Low GI/GL Diet	Wine	
DIY	Pilates	Woodworking	

To order any of these titles, please telephone 0870 787 1732 quoting reference 263H. For further information about all Collins books, visit our website: www.collins.co.uk